HBR Guide to
Getting the
Right Work Done

Harvard Business Review Guides

Arm yourself with the advice you need to succeed on the job, from the most trusted brand in business. Packed with how-to essentials from leading experts, the HBR Guides provide smart answers to your most pressing work challenges.

The titles include:

HBR Guide to Better Business Writing

HBR Guide to Finance Basics for Managers

HBR Guide to Getting the Mentoring You Need

HBR Guide to Getting the Right Job

HBR Guide to Getting the Right Work Done

HBR Guide to Giving Effective Feedback

HBR Guide to Making Every Meeting Matter

HBR Guide to Managing Stress at Work

HBR Guide to Managing Up and Across

HBR Guide to Persuasive Presentations

HBR Guide to Project Management

HBR Guide to
Getting
the Right
Work Done

HARVARD BUSINESS REVIEW PRESS

Boston, Massachusetts

Library of Congress Cataloging-in-Publication Data

HBR guide to getting the right work done.
    p. cm.
  ISBN 978-1-4221-8711-1 (alk. paper)
   1. Time management.   2. Decision making.   I. Harvard Business Review Press.   II. Title: Harvard Business Review guide to getting the right work done.   III. Title: Guide to getting the right work done.
   HD69.T54.H374 2012
   650.1'1—dc23

                                      2012012383

MIX
Paper from responsible sources
FSC www.fsc.org FSC® C101537

What You'll Learn

Are you paralyzed by the pile of projects on your plate? Has fear of delegation buried you in administrivia? Is your focus destroyed by the incessant call of e-mail and Twitter? Do you leave work exhausted—but with little to show for it? Are promotions passing you by because your peers are more productive?

You can't possibly tackle every task that awaits you. But here's the good news: You can learn to get the *right* work done, focusing your time and energy where it'll yield the greatest reward—for you and your organization. This guide will help by offering a range of accessible tools so you can sample them and see what works for you.

You'll get better at:

- Prioritizing

- Staying focused

- Working less but accomplishing more

- Stopping bad habits and developing good ones

- Writing to-do lists that work

- Breaking overwhelming projects into manageable pieces

- Thwarting e-mail overload

- Refueling your energy

Contents

Contents

Section 3: ORGANIZE YOUR TIME

Section 4: DELEGATE EFFECTIVELY

Section 5: CREATE RITUALS

Contents

Section 8: MAINTAIN YOUR NEW APPROACH

Section 9: EXPLORE FURTHER

Section 1
Get Started

Chapter 1
You Can't Get It *All* Done

by Peter Bregman

Brad is as hard a worker as anyone I know. (Names and some details have been changed.) He's not just busy, he's keenly focused on getting the right things done. And it pays off—he is the largest single revenue generator at his well-known professional services firm. A few days before Thanksgiving, Brad flew from Boston to Los Angeles with his family. During the five-hour flight, he decided not to use the plane's Internet access, choosing to play with his children instead. A five-hour digital vacation.

When they landed, Brad turned on his BlackBerry and discovered that a crisis had developed while he was in the air. He had close to five hundred new e-mail messages.

So much for a digital vacation.

The truth is, we can't really get away from it. There's no escaping the nonstop surge of e-mail, text, voice mail, Twitter, Facebook, LinkedIn—and that's just the technology-based stream. How can we ever catch up?

We can't.

The idea that we can get it all done is the biggest myth in time management. There's no way Brad can meaningfully go through all his e-mail, and there's no way any of us are going to accomplish everything we want to.

Face it: You're a limited resource.

On the one hand, that's depressing. On the other hand, acknowledging it can be tremendously empowering. Once we admit that we aren't going to get it *all* done, we're in a much better position to make explicit choices about what we *are* going to do. Instead of letting things haphazardly fall through the cracks, we can intentionally push the unimportant things aside and focus our energy on the things that matter most.

That's what this guide is all about.

There are two main challenges in doing the right things: identifying what they are and then doing them.

To determine the "right things," we need to make choices that will move us toward the outcomes we most want. Which, of course, means we need to know what our priorities are.

In terms of the second challenge—the "doing" or follow-through—we need tools. Rituals. To-do lists. Delegation skills.

But which tools will work best for you? Which rituals will help you follow through? You might be the kind of person who can read through a book like this, full of great advice, and implement it all at once. I am not. I get overwhelmed and end up not changing anything.

So, here's one way to use this guide:

1. **Identify your time management challenges.** Do you leave the office with a nagging feeling that you worked all day but didn't get your most important work done? Are you distracted by little things? Avoiding big, hairy projects? Take this three-minute quiz (see "How well do you manage distraction?") to discover where you're distracting yourself the most.

2. **Find one piece of advice you think will have the greatest impact on your work.** Once you've identified your biggest challenges, read through this guide and find a tip that speaks to you. Maybe you're not clear on your "right things." Maybe the rituals you're using aren't working. Maybe you procrastinate. Choose one tactic you think will help you the most. Then do that *one* thing.

3. **Do it again.** Once that tactic has had an impact on your work, repeat the process. Return to this guide and select another tip.

Because Brad is a paragon of productivity, he decided to put his BlackBerry away and wait to reply to the messages until he was in his hotel room. Then, using his laptop, he attacked the crisis: called his client to allay their concerns, delegated tasks to his team, and sent an e-mail to his team and his client detailing the plan. Within an hour, he had finished, shut his laptop, left his BlackBerry in his room, and enjoyed a fun, chaos-filled dinner with

TABLE 1-1

How well do you manage distraction?

1. Even though it feels like I work nonstop all day, I still don't get the most important things done.	Never	Occasionally	Often	Always
2. No matter what I intend to focus on at the beginning of the day, as soon as I start working (checking e-mail, etc.), I seem to get derailed and lose my focus.	Never	Occasionally	Often	Always
3. When I have something important and challenging I want to accomplish, I spend my time doing lots of little things and avoiding the big one.	Never	Occasionally	Often	Always
4. When my work gets challenging, I somehow keep interrupting myself by surfing the Web, doing e-mail, and other distractions.	Never	Occasionally	Often	Always
5. When I'm on a conference call, I get bored and start multitasking until I miss something important; then I try to recover without making it obvious that I wasn't paying attention.	Never	Occasionally	Often	Always
6. I'm late for meetings and appointments because I try to get one more thing done instead of leaving enough time for preparation and/or travel.	Never	Occasionally	Often	Always
7. I feel overwhelmed and stressed out by the number of things I have to do.	Never	Occasionally	Often	Always
8. My work day ends in frustration as I think about all the things I intended to accomplish but didn't.	Never	Occasionally	Often	Always
9. When I try to make space for my own work, I get interrupted by others and I find it hard to protect my time.	Never	Occasionally	Often	Always
10. I don't spend enough time at work in my "sweet spot" (doing work I'm really good at and enjoy the most).	Never	Occasionally	Often	Always

Score yourself

Number of checks in:

Never _____
Occasionally _____
Often _____
Always _____

Guide to scores

If you selected mostly "Never," congratulations! You're already doing a great job of focusing on the work that will give you—and your organization—the highest reward. You likely already have rituals and tactics that make you productive. Look to this guide for some new tips and ideas to expand your collection of productivity tools.

If you selected mostly "Occasionally," you're doing pretty well. Perhaps willpower or delegating is helping you focus on getting the right work done. But there's even more you could be doing to boost your productivity. Perhaps you haven't experimented with rituals. Perhaps your obsession with e-mail is derailing you. Read on to discover new ideas about how you can get even more of the right work done.

If you selected mostly "Often," you could use a process to help you get and stay focused on the right work. Resist the allure of "urgent" projects to focus on the work with the greatest long-term rewards. Learn how to craft the most useful to-do lists so that you can power through them and leave work feeling a sense of accomplishment.

If you selected mostly "Always," you need help. But you know that, because you bought this guide, so you're already on the path to productivity. Pick your biggest pain point and start there, then return to the Guide as often as you need to.

This quiz is derived from Peter's book, *18 Minutes: Find Your Focus, Master Distractions, and Get the Right Things Done*. For free *18 Minutes* tools and resources (including an online version of this quiz offering more detailed results and feedback), visit http://www.peterbregman.com.

his family—which, at that time, was precisely the right thing for him to do.

———————

Peter Bregman is a strategic adviser to CEOs and their leadership teams. His latest book is *18 Minutes: Find Your Focus, Master Distraction, and Get the Right Things Done.*

Chapter 2
Nine Things Successful People Do Differently

by Heidi Grant Halvorson

Why have you been so successful in reaching some of your goals, but not others? If you aren't sure, you're far from alone. Even brilliant, highly accomplished people are pretty lousy when it comes to understanding why they succeed or fail. The intuitive answer—that you're born predisposed to certain talents and lacking in others— is really just one small piece of the puzzle. In fact, decades of research on achievement suggest that successful people reach their personal and professional goals not

---

Excerpted with permission from *Nine Things Successful People Do Differently* (product #11065).

simply because of who they are, but more often because of what they do.

What follows are the nine things that successful people do—the strategies they use to set and pursue goals (sometimes without consciously realizing it) that have the biggest impact on performance.

1. Get Specific

When you set a goal, be as specific as possible. "Lose five pounds" is a better goal than "lose some weight," because it gives you a clear idea of what success looks like. Knowing exactly what you want to achieve keeps you motivated until you get there. Also, consider the specific actions you'll need to take to reach your goal. Promising you'll "eat less" or "sleep more" is too vague. "I'll be in bed by 10 PM on weeknights" leaves no doubt about what you need to do, and whether or not you've actually done it.

Spelling out exactly what you want to achieve removes the possibility of settling for less—of telling yourself that what you've done is "good enough." It also makes your course of action clearer.

Instead of "getting ahead at work," make your goal more concrete, such as "a pay raise of at least $ _____" or "a promotion to at least the _____ level."

To be successful, you also need to get specific about the obstacles you may encounter. In fact, what you really need to do is go back and forth, thinking about the success you want to achieve and the steps it will take to get there. This strategy is called **mental contrasting,** and it's a remarkably effective way to set goals and strengthen your commitment.

To use the mental contrasting technique, first imagine how you'll feel attaining your goal. Picture it as vividly as you can—really consider the details. Next, think about the obstacles in your way. For instance, if you wanted to get a better, higher-paying job, you would start by imagining the sense of pride and excitement you would feel accepting a lucrative offer at a top firm. Then you would think about what stands between you and that offer— namely, all the other really outstanding candidates. Kind of makes you want to polish up your résumé a bit, doesn't it?

That's called **experiencing the necessity to act;** it's a state that's critical for reaching your goal, because it gets the psychological wheels in motion. Mental contrasting turns wishes and desires into reality by bringing attention and clarity to what you will need to do to make them happen.

2. Seize the Moment to Act on Your Goals

Given how busy most of us are and how many things we're juggling at once, it's not surprising that we routinely miss opportunities to act on a goal. Did you really have no time to work out today? No chance at any point to return that phone call?

To seize the moment, decide when and where you'll take action, in advance. Be specific ("If it's Monday, Wednesday, or Friday, I'll work out for thirty minutes before work"). Studies show that this **if-then planning** helps your brain to detect and take advantage of the opportunity when it arises, increasing your chances of success by roughly 300 percent. (For more on planning when and where you'll perform tasks, see "How to Tackle Your To-Do List," later in this guide.)

Deciding in advance when and where you will take specific actions to reach your goal (or how you will address obstacles you might encounter) is probably the most effective single thing you can do to ensure your success.

If-then plans take the form:

If X happens, then I will do Y.

For example:

If I'm getting too distracted by colleagues, then I'll stick to a five-minute chat limit and return to work.

Why are these plans so effective? Because they're written in the language of your brain—the language of contingencies. Humans are particularly good at encoding and remembering information in "if X, then Y" terms, and using these contingencies to guide their behavior, often below their level of awareness.

Once you've formulated your if-then plan, your unconscious brain will start scanning the environment, searching for the situation in the "if" part of your plan. This enables you to seize the critical moment ("Oh, it's 4 PM! I'd better return those calls!"), even when you're busy doing other things.

Since you've already decided exactly what you need to do, you can execute the plan without having to consciously think about it.

3. Know Exactly How Far You Have Left to Go

Achieving any goal also requires honest and regular monitoring of your progress—if not by others, then by you yourself. If you don't know how well you're doing, you can't adjust your behavior or your strategies accordingly. Check your progress frequently—weekly, or even daily, depending on the goal.

Feedback helps motivate us because we subconsciously tune in to the presence of a discrepancy between where we are now and where we want to be. When your brain detects a discrepancy, it reacts by throwing resources at it: attention, effort, deeper processing of information, and willpower.

If self-monitoring and seeking out feedback are so important, you may be wondering why we don't always do it. The first and most obvious reason is that it's effortful; you need to stop whatever else you're doing and really focus on assessment. And of course, the news isn't always positive; sometimes we avoid checking in on our progress because we don't want to acknowledge how little progress we've made. Self-monitoring requires a lot of willpower, but you can make it easier by using if-then planning to schedule your self-assessments.

Done the right way, assessing your progress will keep you motivated from start to finish. Done the wrong way, it may actually lower your motivation. Recent research by University of Chicago psychologists Minjung Koo and Ayelet Fishbach examined how people pursuing goals were affected by focusing on either how far they had already come (**to-date thinking**) or what was left to be ac-complished (**to-go thinking**).

Koo and Fishbach's studies consistently show that when we're pursuing a goal and consider how far we've already come, we feel a premature sense of accomplish-ment and begin to slack off.

When we focus on progress made, we're also more likely to try to achieve a sense of "balance" by making progress on other important goals. As a result, we wind up with lots of pots on the stove, but nothing is ever ready to eat.

If, instead, we focus on how far we have left to go (to-go thinking), motivation is not only sustained, it's heightened. So when you're assessing your progress, stay focused on the goal and never congratulate yourself too much on a job half-done. Save it for a job well—and completely—done.

4. Be a Realistic Optimist

When you're setting a goal, by all means engage in posi-tive thinking about how likely you are to achieve it. Be-lieving in your ability to succeed is enormously helpful for creating and sustaining your motivation. But don't underestimate the time, planning, effort, and persistence it will take to reach your goal. Thinking things will come to you easily and effortlessly leaves you ill prepared for the journey ahead and can significantly increase the odds of failure.

This is the difference between being a realistic opti-mist and an unrealistic optimist.

Realistic optimists believe they will succeed, but also believe they have to make success happen—through things like planning, persistence, and choosing the right strategies. They recognize the need for considering how they'll deal with obstacles.

Unrealistic optimists, on the other hand, believe that success will happen to them—that the universe will reward them for their positive thinking.

Cultivate your realistic optimism by combining a positive attitude with an honest assessment of the challenges that await you. Don't just visualize success; visualize the steps you will take in order to make success happen. If your first strategy doesn't work, what's plan B? (This is another great time to use your if-then plans.) Remember, it's not "negative" to think about the problems you are likely to face—it's foolish not to.

5. Focus on Getting Better, Rather Than Being Good

Believing you have the ability to reach your goals is important, but so is believing you can *get* the ability. Many of us believe that our intelligence, personality, and physical aptitudes are fixed—that no matter what we do, we won't improve. As a result, we focus on goals that are all about proving ourselves, rather than developing and acquiring new skills.

Fortunately, **abilities of all kinds are profoundly malleable.** Embracing the fact that you can change will allow you to make better choices and reach your fullest potential. People whose goals are about getting better, rather than being good, take difficulty in stride and appreciate the journey as much as the destination.

How can you motivate yourself to approach new responsibilities with confidence and energy? The answer is simple, though perhaps a little surprising: **give yourself permission to screw up.**

I know this may not be something you're thrilled to hear, because you're probably thinking, if you screw up you'll be the one to pay for it. But you needn't worry, because when people feel they're allowed to make mistakes, they're significantly less likely to actually make them!

People approach any task with one of two types of goals: what I call **be-good goals,** where the focus is on proving that you have a lot of ability and already know what you're doing, and **get-better goals,** where the focus is on developing ability and learning to master a new skill.

The problem with be-good goals is that they tend to backfire when we're faced with something unfamiliar or difficult. We quickly start feeling that we don't actually know what we're doing, that we lack ability—and this creates a lot of anxiety. And nothing interferes with performance quite like anxiety does; it is *the* productivity killer.

Get-better goals, on the other hand, are practically bulletproof. When we think about what we're doing in terms of learning and mastering—accepting that we may make some mistakes along the way—we stay motivated despite setbacks that might occur.

A focus on getting better also enhances the experience of working; we naturally find what we do more interesting and enjoyable when we think about it in terms of progress, rather than perfection. Finding what you do interesting and believing it has inherent value is one of the most effective ways to stay motivated despite unexpected roadblocks. In fact, interest doesn't just keep you going despite fatigue; it actually replenishes your energy.

6. Have Grit

Grit is a willingness to commit to long-term goals and to persist in the face of difficulty. Gritty people obtain more education in their lifetimes and earn higher college GPAs. Grit predicts which cadets will stick out their first grueling year at West Point. In fact, grit even predicts how far contestants at the Scripps National Spelling Bee will go.

The good news is that if you aren't particularly gritty now, you can do something about it. People who lack grit often believe that they just don't have the innate abilities successful people have. If that describes your own thinking, you're wrong. As I mentioned earlier, effort, planning, persistence, and good strategies are what it really takes to succeed. Embracing this knowledge will not only help you see yourself and your goals more accurately, but also do wonders for your grit.

Study after study of successful people, whether they are athletes, musicians, or mathematicians, shows that the key to success and enhanced ability is deliberate practice—thousands of hours spent mastering the necessary skills and knowledge.

Grit is all about not giving up in the face of difficulty, even when you're tired or discouraged. And the best predictor of not giving up is how we explain that difficulty in the first place. When you're having a hard time, what do you blame?

Entity theorists, who are convinced that ability is fixed, tend to **blame setbacks on a lack of ability.** If this is hard for me, I must not be good at it. As a result, they lack grit; they give up on themselves way too soon, inadvertently reinforcing their misconception that they can't improve.

Incremental theorists, on the other hand, tend to **blame setbacks on more controllable factors**—insufficient effort, using the wrong strategy, poor planning. When faced with difficulty, they try harder, armed with the belief that improvement is always possible. This gritty attitude leads to far greater long-term accomplishments.

Change really is always possible, and the science here is crystal clear. There is no ability that can't be developed with experience. The next time you find yourself thinking, "But I'm just not good at this," remember: You're just not good at it *yet*.

7. Build Your Willpower Muscle

Our self-control "muscle" is just like others in your body; when it doesn't get much exercise, it becomes weaker over time. But when you give it regular workouts, it will grow stronger and help you reach your goals.

To build willpower, take on a challenge that requires you to do something you'd rather not do. Give up high-fat snacks, do a hundred sit-ups a day, try to learn a new skill. When you find yourself wanting to give in or give up—don't. Start with just one activity and make a plan for how you'll deal with troubles when they occur ("If I want a snack, I'll eat one piece of fresh or three pieces of dried fruit"). It will be hard in the beginning, but it will get easier, and that's the whole point. As your strength grows, you can take on more challenges and step up your self-control workout.

Like biceps or triceps, willpower can vary in its strength, not only from person to person, but from moment to moment.

The good news is that willpower depletion is only temporary. Give your muscle time to bounce back, and you'll be back in fighting form. When rest is not an option, you can accelerate your recovery simply by thinking about people you know who have a lot of self-control.

Or, you can try giving yourself a pick-me-up. Anything that lifts your spirits—listening to a favorite song, calling a good friend, or reflecting on a past success—should also help restore your self-control when you're looking for a quick fix.

8. Don't Tempt Fate

No matter how strong your willpower muscle becomes, it's important to always respect the fact that it's limited, and if you overtax it, you will temporarily run out of steam. Don't try to take on two challenging goals at once, if you can help it (like quitting smoking *and* dieting). And make achieving your goal easier by keeping yourself out of harm's way. Many people are overly confident in their ability to resist temptation, and as a result they put themselves in situations where temptations abound. Successful people know not to make reaching a goal harder than it already is.

Resisting temptation is a key part of successfully reaching just about any goal. What we want to do is often the very opposite of what we need to do. This may sound a bit counterintuitive, but the very first thing you're going to want to do if you're serious about resisting temptation is **make peace with the fact that your willpower is limited.**

Even if you've built up large reserves of willpower, you won't have much left for sticking to your resolutions at the end of a long day of putting out fires at work. That's why it's so important to give some thought to when you're most likely to feel drained and vulnerable and make an if-then plan to keep yourself out of harm's way.

It's far easier to abstain from doing something all together than it is to give in just a little and then stop. And you need more and more self-control to stop a behavior the longer it goes on. If you don't want to eat the entire slice of cake, don't take "just one bite."

9. Focus on What You Will Do, Not What You Won't Do

Do you want to get promoted, quit smoking, or put a lid on your bad temper? Then plan how you'll replace counterproductive behaviors with more constructive ones. Too often, people concentrate all their efforts on what they want to stop doing and fail to consider how they will fill the void. Trying to avoid a thought can make it more active in your mind ("Don't think about white bears!"). The same holds true when it comes to behavior; by trying not to do something, you strengthen rather than diminish the impulse.

If you want to change your ways, ask yourself, "What will I do instead?" For example, if you're trying to gain control of your temper, you might make a plan such as, "If I'm starting to feel angry, then I'll take three deep breaths to calm down." By using deep breathing as a replacement for giving in to your anger, your success-sabotaging impulse will get worn away over time until it disappears completely.

Once you've decided to make an if-then plan to help you reach your goal, the next thing you need to do is figure out how to construct it.

There are three types of if-then plans:

- **"Replacement" if-then plans** do just what the name suggests—replace a negative behavior with a more positive one (as in the anger management strategy just described).

- **"Ignore" if-then plans** are focused on blocking out unwanted feelings, like cravings, performance anxiety, or self-doubts. ("If I have the urge to smoke, then I'll ignore it.")

- Finally, **"negation" if-then plans** involve spelling out the actions you won't be taking in the future. With these plans, if there is a behavior you want to avoid, you simply plan not to perform this behavior. ("If I am at the mall, then I won't buy anything.")

Of all three types, replacement plans are most successful. When it comes to reaching your goals, focusing on what you *will* do, not what you *won't* do, is the most effective way to achieve them.

––––––––––––––

Heidi Grant Halvorson, PhD, is a motivational psychologist and author of the HBR Single *Nine Things Successful People Do Differently* (Harvard Business Press, 2011) and the book *Succeed: How We Can Reach Our Goals* (Hudson Street Press, 2011). Her personal blog, *The Science of Success,* can be found at http://www.heidigranthalvorson .com/.

Chapter 3
Being More Productive

An Interview with David Allen and Tony Schwartz

by Daniel McGinn

David Allen is a productivity consultant and the author of the best seller *Getting Things Done,* which outlines the list-driven efficiency system adherents call by its acronym: GTD. Tony Schwartz, the author of the best-seller *Be Excellent at Anything,* is the CEO of The Energy Project, which helps people and organizations fuel engagement and productivity by drawing on the science of high performance.

Excerpted from *Harvard Business Review,* May 2011 (product # R1105D).

In this edited conversation with HBR, they discuss the distractive pull of e-mail, how they've been influenced by each other, and why you should do your most important task first thing in the morning (even though only one of them does).

HBR: Let's start with something simple. How does each of you define what you do?

Allen: I help people and organizations produce more with less input. I teach a set of best practices and a methodology that produce a greater sense of concentration and control.

Schwartz: We teach individuals and organizations how to manage energy more skillfully in order to get more work done in less time, more sustainably. That requires a new way of working—one that balances periods of high focus with intermittent renewal.

Both of you have written several books describing your techniques, but give me a quick summary.

Allen: I call what I've uncovered "the strategic value of clear space." Say you're going to cook dinner for people, it's 5:00 PM, and they're coming at 6:00. You want to have all the right ingredients. You want to have the right tools. You want the kitchen to be nice and clear. You need the freedom to make a creative mess. I teach people to achieve that freedom by taking very immediate, concrete steps: downloading all your commitments and projects into lists, focusing on "next actions," and thinking about the context—work that needs to be done in your office, or on the phone, or on the computer. You don't need to change who you are. You just need some simple but very powerful techniques.

Schwartz: We focus on the four primary dimensions of energy that we all need to perform at our best. The ground level is physical—fitness, sleep, nutrition, and rest. At the emotional level, it's about cultivating positive emotions—and as a leader, communicating them to others. At the mental level, it's about gaining more control of your attention—both by increasing [your] ability to focus on one thing at a time and by learning to shift into the right hemisphere to do more-creative work. And at the spiritual level, it's about defining purpose, because when something really matters, you bring far more energy to it. Very few [managers and] leaders I've met fully appreciate how meeting these needs—in themselves and for others—is absolutely critical to sustainable high performance. They're good at doing things, and they've been rewarded by being given more things to do. But increasingly, demand is outrunning their capacity. They're overloaded with e-mail and texts and all the information that comes in. We have to teach them to step back and say, "What do I actually want to do? What are the right choices? What are the costs of this choice?"

Let's talk about some of the concrete principles you teach. Tony, explain why you think people should

approach work as a series of short sprints, not an all-day marathon.

Schwartz: There's a fundamental misunderstanding about how human beings operate at their best. Most of us mistakenly assume we're meant to run like computers—at high speeds, continuously, for long periods of time, running multiple programs simultaneously. It's just not true. Human beings are designed to be *rhythmic.* The heart pulses; muscles contract and relax. We're at our best when we're moving rhythmically between spending energy and renewing it. We need to recognize the insight of athletes, who manage their work-rest ratios. We encourage people to work intensely for 90 minutes and then take a break to recover. We teach them to eat small, energy-rich meals every few hours, rather than three big meals a day. We believe napping drives productivity, although that remains a tough sell in most companies. Still, the reality is that if a person works continuously all through the day, she'll produce less than a person of equal talent who works very intensely for short periods and then recovers before working intensely again. (To learn more, see "Power Through Your Day in 90-Minute Cycles" and "Manage Your Energy, Not Your Time," later in this guide.)

Allen: It's also an issue of choosing the right work. Peter Drucker said that the toughest job for knowledge workers is defining the work. A century ago, 80% of the world made and moved things. You worked as long as you could, and then you slept, and then you got up and worked again. You didn't have to triage or make executive decisions. It's harder to be productive today because the work has become much more complex.

David, what's the biggest roadblock to productivity that you typically observe when you go into an organization for the first time?

Allen: People don't capture stuff that has their attention. They don't acknowledge it or objectify it. And it keeps rolling around in the organizational psyche as well as the personal psyche, draining energy and creating incredible psychic residue. People say, "I'll do that," but they don't write it down, and it goes into a black hole. That would be fine if it were just one thing, but it's hundreds of things. And people don't determine exactly what their commitment to that stuff is—what's the outcome they want to achieve, what's the next action required to move it forward. Your head is for having ideas, not holding them. Just dumping everything out of your head and externalizing it is a huge step, and it can have a significant effect.

The devil's advocate position is that this results in gigantic to-do lists, which are overwhelming in themselves.

Allen: You need lists because your brain isn't good at keeping them. Your mind is this dumb little computer that will wake you up at 3:00 AM and beat you bloody over stuff you can't do spit about while you're lying there. All it's doing is repeating stuff in open loops, and it sucks your energy like crazy.

Schwartz: There's a process of humility that's required here. It's a little bit of a turn on the 12-step notion of admitting that you're powerless over your addictions. In this case, the addiction is to e-mail and information. The problem is that our willpower and self-discipline are wildly overrated. We think the way to make a change is to push harder—to resist that chocolate-chip cookie, or wake up early and get to the gym. It doesn't work. It's humbling to discover that we're creatures of habit, and what we did yesterday is what we're going to do today. You want to co-opt the process by which negative habits arise without your intention, and substitute what we call "positive rituals," or deliberate practices. (See Section 5: Create Rituals.)

How much do you know about each other's work—and how much do you use each other's strategies?

Schwartz: I always kept lists, but until I connected with David's work, I didn't realize that anything I didn't download would potentially create distractions—so now I keep lists of *everything*. Another ritual I have that aligns with David's work is to always do the most important task of the day first thing in the morning, when I'm most rested and least distracted. Ninety percent of people check their e-mail as soon as they get to work. That turns their agenda over to someone else.

David, how has Tony's thinking influenced the way you work?

Allen: The piece that's made the biggest difference is his work on energy cycles. I actually brought a pillow into work. I work in a glass office, and now people can see me lying on my floor taking a nap for 20 minutes. That's directly from Tony's work. I wish I had the discipline Tony does to tackle the hardest tasks first thing in the morning, but I don't.

Schwartz: It's not that you don't have the discipline— it's that you don't have the ritual. If you built that ritual, I have zero doubt that you could do it.

Allen: Part of the way to attack that problem is to break big tasks down and focus on smaller "next actions," which can seem more manageable. What most people put on a to-do list are vague things like "Mom." Great! So Tony will write down "Mom," signifying that he has to decide whether to get his mother a birthday present, and what to buy, and how to deliver it. He'll resist looking at the list, because he knows there's a lot of work in that simple notation. Instead the list should specify a smaller next action—say, "Call sister re: Mom's birthday." Oh, look—I can do that! There's actually a part of us that loves to produce, that loves to be complete. Now I've created motivation: I see a desired result, I have the confidence I can get there, and I see the path. A lot of what GTD does is set it up so that you only have to think about things once. The problem is that everybody is multitasking and getting distracted by the latest and loudest. They fail because they haven't captured, clarified, organized, or built in a regular review system they trust.

Schwartz: Let me beg to differ a little. Say you're working on a primary task and you get an e-mail. You hear that little Pavlovian beep, and you cannot resist it. So you turn to the e-mail and lose track of the initial task, and it takes you time to reconnect to it afterward. Researchers have found that over time and with practice, people get better at task shifting, but they never get remotely as good as they'd be if they did one thing at a time. (For more on effective to-do lists and multitasking, see Section 3: Organize Your Time.)

Allen: Let's take it a step further. Why do people get disturbed by that e-mail beep? It's because they don't trust that they've emptied their e-mail every 24 hours. Most people are living in an emergency scan mode. They never deal with their e-mail, so they're afraid there's still something sitting in there, and they're constantly allowing themselves to get distracted by it. (See Section 7: Take Control of Your E-mail.)

Last question: If people could take just one thing away from your work, what should it be?

Schwartz: [We] need to recognize that human beings are basically organisms containing energy. And that energy is either being renewed or being dissipated over time. An organization has to realize that part of its responsibility, whether it wants it or not, is to ensure that people have full tanks of energy. This is one of the big variables that will determine which organizations thrive in the next 10 or 20 years. [And until organizations do so, we need to take on that responsibility for ourselves.]

Allen: Think about it this way: While we've been sitting here talking, stuff has been piling up in our in-boxes and our voice mails. Some of it has the potential to meaningfully shift our priorities. When we turn to this accumulated stuff, we'll need to eliminate old business that is pulling on us, that's taking our attention, and reallocate our resources to these new priorities. You can only do one thing at a time, and you only have so many resources. You either feel OK about sitting here talking to us, or you feel bad about the 9,000 other things you're not doing. Everybody needs a system to make those choices wisely.

Daniel McGinn is a senior editor at *Harvard Business Review*.

Section 2
Prioritize Your Work

Chapter 4
Get a Raise by Getting the Right Work Done

by Peter Bregman

My friend Dave is notorious for eating fried food. (Names and some details changed.) Yet recently he was surprised to learn that his cholesterol was high because, as he put it, "The day before the test, I ate really well."

The idea of immediate results is alluring. But whether it's managing our diet or prioritizing our workload, there are no quick fixes.

I was reminded of this when a reporter asked me what advice I would give to someone who wanted to ask for a raise at a time when most wages are stagnating or falling. My answer? Don't ask.

It's not that I think people can't get raises right now. But if you haven't spent the last year laying the groundwork, it's highly unlikely that you'll be successful now. There's no formula—no perfect words or spinning of events—that will magically deliver a raise with a day or two of preparation.

But there is a formula for getting more money over time. And it starts with your ability to prioritize.

The formula is based on one simple premise: We can get more money when we demonstrate that we've added more value. And we can add more value when we spend the majority of our time focusing on the work that the most senior leaders in our organization *consider* valuable, which is almost always work that increases revenue or profits, either short-term or long-term.

But when we're not clear about what work is most important to our organization, one of two things can happen: Either we put the same amount of energy and effort into everything or we let the wrong things fall through the cracks.

Making more intentional and strategic choices about where to spend our time can mean the difference between a stagnant salary and a growing one. We can be more productive when we know which initiatives deserve our highest priority.

Here's my formula for getting a raise:

1. During this year's compensation conversation, take whatever is given to you without negotiation and with appreciation. Then explain that you're less interested in a raise right now and more interested in **how you can add tremendous value to the organization.**

2. Think like a shareholder of the company. Ask lots of questions about the strategy and what's keeping the top leaders awake at night. Understand how your department affects revenue or profitability and what's important to your direct manager. With your manager, identify the top two or three things you can work on that will drive revenue or profitability. Once you've had that conversation, **you'll have your raiseworthy work focus.**

3. Now **keep those two or three revenue and/or profitability drivers at the top of your to-do list.** Approach your daily work so that the majority of your effort moves the organization further in those areas. Share your to-do list with your manager, to keep you on the same page about your priorities and how your work affects the bigger picture. Quantify the impact you're making. If your manager asks you to do things outside of your top priorities, push back and discuss the possible trade-offs you could make. Sure, you'll need to work on some things that aren't important. But make a strategic choice to shortchange those.

After about six months of this laser focus, you'll be ready to talk about how you've added tremendous value on the things that matter most.

During that discussion you'll also be ready to talk about a real raise. That's good timing, since most organizations are beginning to think through their departmental budgets and promotions around the six-month mark.

Here's why this formula works: It's not a trick. If you focus on your highest-priority work—even if it requires that you push back when your manager asks you to work on other tasks—ultimately you and your manager will be more productive, and the organization will benefit. That's money in the bank. It will make your job more secure and you more promotable.

"So," I asked Dave. "Now that you know you have high cholesterol, are you going to change the way you eat?"

"No," Dave answered, true to form, "I'm taking a pill. My cholesterol will be lower in a few days and I can still eat everything."

Maybe I like doing things the hard way. But as far as I know, there's no pill for getting a raise.

Peter Bregman is a strategic adviser to CEOs and their leadership teams. His latest book is *18 Minutes: Find Your Focus, Master Distraction, and Get the Right Things Done.*

Chapter 5
The Worth-Your-Time Test

by Peter Bregman

Nate Eisman recently started working for a large consulting firm after many years as an independent consultant. (Some details changed to protect privacy.) He called me for some advice.

"I'm wasting a tremendous amount of time," he complained. "I'm in meetings all day. The only way I can get any real work done is by coming in super early and staying super late."

Nate had gone from an organization of one to an organization of several thousand and was drowning in the time suck of collaboration. He is not alone.

Working with people takes time. And different people have different priorities. Someone may need your per-

---

Adapted from content posted on hbr.org on April 1, 2010.

spective on an issue that's critical to him but not to you. Still, if he's a colleague, it's important to help. And often, we want to help.

On the other hand, we've all felt Nate's pain: How can we spend time where we add the most value and let go of the rest?

We need a way to quickly and confidently identify and reduce our extraneous commitments, to know for sure whether we need to deal with something or delegate it, and to manage our desire to be available to others. I propose a brief test that every commitment should pass before you agree to it. When someone comes to you with a request, ask yourself:

1. Am I the right person?

2. Is this the right time?

3. Do I have enough information?

If the request fails the test—if the answer to any one of these questions is "no"—then don't do it. Pass it to someone else (the right person), schedule it for another time (the right time), or wait until you have the information you need (either you or someone else needs to get it).

Sometimes it's impossible or inappropriate to wall yourself off completely. For example, what if your boss is the person who interrupts you? Or what if you're on vacation and an important client reaches out with a time-sensitive and crucial question?

The three test questions offer a clear, easy, and consistent way of knowing how to respond—and help us avoid the tendency to say yes to everything.

If your boss asks you to do something and her request fails the test, it's not just okay, it's *useful* to push back on or redirect her so the work is completed productively. It's not helpful to you, your boss, or your organization if you waste your time on the wrong work.

That's the irony. We try to be available because we want to be helpful. And yet being overwhelmed with tasks—especially those we consider to be a waste of our time—is exactly what will make us unhelpful.

When we get a meeting request that doesn't pass the test, we should decline it. When we're cc'd on an e-mail that doesn't require our attention, we need to delete it. And a 50-page presentation needs to pass the test before we read it—and even then, it's worth an e-mail asking which are the critical pages to review.

A few weeks after sharing the three questions with Nate, I called him at his office at around 6 PM to see how it was going. I guess it was going well, because I never reached him. He had already gone home.

Peter Bregman is a strategic adviser to CEOs and their leadership teams. His latest book is *18 Minutes: Find Your Focus, Master Distraction, and Get the Right Things Done.*

Chapter 6
Say Yes to Saying No

by Alexandra Samuel

If your e-mail in-box looks like mine, it's full of requests and invitations that promise challenging new projects, clients, and commitments. Sure, you enjoy the stimulation and excitement that come with these offers, but it's a fine line. You have to be selective about what you take on—and disciplined about retiring long-standing activities to make room for new ones. You have to be able to say no. Frequently, politely, and effectively.

The good news is that the same technologies that threaten to overload you with things to say yes to can also help you say no. Here's how:

Adapted from content posted on hbr.org on January 8, 2010.

Set your intentions

Before you say no, make it clear to yourself what you want to say yes to. Sites like 43Things.com and SuperViva .com can help you create lists of what you want to accomplish and experiences you want to have. Writing down your goals will help you clarify what's important, identify what you want to eliminate, and get the community support to achieve it.

Prioritize your commitments

A simple Excel spreadsheet can help you evaluate what's on your plate before you agree to take on more. Capture every project you're working on—even ones you've only thought about—and list these in column A, one row per task. Use column B to assign a priority to each project, ranking items from 1–5. In column C, capture the name of anyone who could take over or help with certain projects. Sort your projects according to priority.

For high-priority tasks you've noted could be delegated, e-mail or meet with everyone to whom you hope to transfer projects.

Review with your boss the list of high-priority tasks that only you can handle. Are they aligned with her and your unit's goals? If not, reevaluate to see if you should: shift priorities; delegate more of the projects; or defer some to a later date. (To download a sample Excel spreadsheet, visit my website at http://www.alexandrasamuel .com/career-work/excel-template-7-steps-to-achieving-your-goals.)

Make it easy to say "no"

When my in-box piles up with unanswered messages, you can bet that it's full of e-mails that require a no—ones that I can't bring myself to write. To make it easier, I've created a few different signature files in my e-mail client, with polite "no" messages for different circumstances: *I'd love to join you, but my schedule is really booked for the next month;* or *Thanks for thinking of us, but we're only taking on XYZ type of client right now;* or *That sounds like a great project, but my pro bono work is already committed for this quarter.* Using these removes the burden of working up the energy to let someone down.

Make "no" your default answer

Say no to the majority of invitations and project offers you receive unless they meet a short set of criteria. For example, I look for conferences that combine business development (getting clients), professional development (improving skills or knowledge), and personal development (regeneration or personal growth), and attend only events that promise meaningful value on at least two of those fronts. Write down your criteria and stick them to your computer monitor, or put them on a digital sticky note.

None of these practices will eliminate the anxiety that comes from saying no or the fear that you may be passing up a fantastic opportunity. But it's because saying no is so difficult that we need tools and systems to make it a little easier and a little more habitual. The more you say no, the better you'll be able to focus on your most important work.

Alexandra Samuel is the Director of the Social + Interactive Media Centre at Emily Carr University, and the cofounder of Social Signal, a Vancouver-based social media agency. You can follow Alex on Twitter at @awsamuel or her blog at alexandrasamuel.com.

Section 3
Organize Your Time

Chapter 7
A Practical Plan for When You Feel Overwhelmed

by Peter Bregman

We've all experienced it: that feeling that we've got so much to do that there's no chance we'll get it all done. And certainly not done on time. Right now, I'm feeling completely overwhelmed by my to-do list.

Here's the crazy part. I just spent the last two days *trying* to work without actually working. I start something but get distracted by the Internet. Or a phone call. Or an e-mail. At a time when I need to be most efficient, I've become less efficient than ever.

You'd think it would be the opposite—that when we have a lot to do, we'd become very productive in order to get it done. Sometimes that happens.

Adapted from content posted on hbr.org on September 23, 2010.

But often, when there's so much competing for our attention, we don't know where to begin—so we don't begin anywhere.

Next time you find yourself in this situation, try this approach:

1. **Write down everything you have to do on a piece of paper.** Resist the urge to use technology for this task. Why? I'm not sure, but somehow writing on paper—and then crossing things out—creates momentum.

2. **Spend 15 minutes completing as many of the easiest, fastest tasks on your list as you can.** Make your quick phone calls. Send your short e-mails. Don't worry about whether these are the most important tasks on your list. You're moving. The goal is to cross off as many tasks as possible in the shortest time. Use a timer to keep you focused.

3. **Work on the most daunting task for the next 35 minutes without interruption.** Turn off your phone, close all the unnecessary windows on your computer, and choose the most challenging task on your list, the one that instills the most stress or is the highest priority. *Then work on it and only it*—without hesitation or distraction—for 35 minutes.

4. **Take a break for 10 minutes, then begin the cycle again.** After 35 minutes of focused work, take

a break. Then start the hourlong process over again, beginning with the 15 minutes of quick actions.

"Thirty years ago," Anne Lamott writes in her book *Bird by Bird*, "my older brother, who was ten years old at the time, was trying to get a report on birds written that he'd had three months to write. It was due the next day. We were out at our family cabin in Bolinas, and he was at the kitchen table close to tears, surrounded by binder paper and pencils and unopened books on birds, immobilized by the hugeness of the task ahead. Then my father sat down beside him, put his arm around my brother's shoulder, and said, 'Bird by bird, buddy. Just take it bird by bird.'"

That's it. *Bird by bird, starting with a bunch of easy birds to help you feel accomplished and then tackling a hard one to gain serious traction and reduce your stress level.* All timed.

Working within a specific and limited time frame is important because the **race against time keeps you focused.** When stress is generalized and diffuse, it's hard to manage. Using a short time frame actually increases the pressure but keeps your effort specific and particular to a single task. That increases good, motivating stress while reducing negative, disconcerting stress. So the fog of feeling overwhelmed dissipates, and forward movement becomes possible.

In practice, I'm finding that although I make myself work at least the full 35 minutes, I don't *always* stop when the 35 minutes of hard work are over, because I'm in the middle of something and I have traction. On the other hand, though it's tempting, I don't exceed the 15 minutes of easy, fast work. When the timer stops, so do I, immediately transitioning to the hard work.

Maybe this method has been working simply because it's novel for me and, like a new diet, offers some structure to motivate my effort. Today, though, it doesn't matter, because it's a useful tool for me. And I'll keep using it until I don't need it or it stops working.

Am I still stressed? Sure. But overwhelmed? Much less so. Because I'm crossing things off my list and getting somewhere on my little tasks as well as my big ones, bird by bird.

Peter Bregman is a strategic adviser to CEOs and their leadership teams. His latest book is *18 Minutes: Find Your Focus, Master Distraction, and Get the Right Things Done.*

Chapter 8
Stop Procrastinating— Now

by Amy Gallo

It seems that no one is immune to procrastination. When someone asked Ernest Hemingway how to write a novel, he replied, "First you defrost the refrigerator." But putting off tasks takes a big toll on our productivity and our psyche.

Here are five principles to follow the next time you find yourself procrastinating:

1. Figure Out What's Holding You Back

When you find yourself ignoring or delaying a task, ask yourself why. Psychiatrist Ned Hallowell says there are two types of tasks we most often defer:

Adapted from content posted on hbr.org on October 11, 2011.

- **Something you don't like to do.** This is the most common one. As Hallowell says, "You don't put off eating your favorite dessert."

- **Something you don't know how to do.** When you lack the necessary knowledge or are unsure of how to start a job, you're more likely to avoid it.

Once you've identified why you've put something off, you can break the cycle and prevent future bouts of procrastination.

2. Set Deadlines

One of the simplest things to do is create a schedule with clear due dates for each task. "As soon as you get the project, chunk it down into a few manageable segments," advises Teresa Amabile, coauthor of *The Progress Principle*. Then, assign deadlines for each task. "Put an appointment in your calendar to work on a small piece of the next segment each day to allow yourself to get it done a bit at a time," she says. These "small wins" make the work more manageable and contribute to your sense of progress. And achieving them is much easier than trying to barrel through a complex project.

Use whatever visual cues work for you: Set reminders in your calendar, add items to your to-do list, or put a sticky note on your computer screen.

3. Increase the Rewards

We often dally because the reward for doing an assignment is too far off. To make a task feel more urgent, focus on short-term rewards. If you always procrastinate on filing your taxes, for example, focus on getting a refund by a certain date. And if there aren't any obvious rewards, create your own. Treat yourself to a coffee break or a quick chat with a coworker once you've finished a task. Embed the reward into the work by making it more fun to do, like partnering with a colleague on a particularly difficult project.

4. Involve Others

One of the principles Hallowell emphasizes is "Never worry alone." If you don't know how to do something, ask for help. Turn to a trusted colleague or a friend for advice. Asking people to review your work can also help spur you to get started, because you know they're expecting it.

5. Get in the Habit

"People throw up a hand and say 'I'm such a procrastinator' as if they have no control," says Hallowell. "You do have control over this, and you'll be very proud when you change it." There are immediate benefits when you start getting things done right away, and it's a habit you can cultivate. Amabile suggests tracking your improvement. "Spend just five minutes a day to note the progress you made, any setbacks you encountered, and what you might do the next day to enable further progress," she says. She recommends you do this in a work diary (see "Use a 10-Minute Diary to Stay on Track," later in this guide). Then see yourself—and talk about yourself with others—as someone who gets things done. "The most powerful event for maintaining positive inner work life is making progress in meaningful work," says Amabile.

———————

Amy Gallo is a contributing editor at *Harvard Business Review*. Follow her on Twitter at @amyegallo.

Chapter 9
Don't Let Long-Term Projects Become Last-Minute Panic

by Peter Bregman

I want to write a screenplay.

Actually, I wanted to write one last year, but then other work took more time than I expected, and I kept pushing "Write screenplay" off my to-do list.

I know I'm not alone in struggling to make incremental progress on long-term projects or goals. How *do* you get started when you have "all the time in the world"?

Maybe you have no due date, like my screenplay. Or maybe you have a deadline that's months away—like preparing a speech, developing a business plan, or designing a training program. Perhaps you tend to procrastinate on projects with generous schedules—until "next month" becomes "next week" and then "next day," and suddenly your long-term project has morphed into a short-term, panic-filled nightmare.

Accomplishing something big and important is rarely as simple as just getting it done. Often we don't know how to start and, even when we do, we rarely have all the knowledge and skills we need to see it through. Also, we always have more urgent things to do and so we push off long-term goals. (See the previous article, "Stop Procrastinating—Now," for more ideas about overcoming the temptation to postpone work.)

We all know the basic advice: Break the work into smaller, more manageable chunks; focus on the next small step; set intermediate deadlines.

It's good advice. But, in my experience, it's not enough.

The reason we procrastinate on a big, long-term project is because it's important. So important, we're too scared to work on it.

I've never written a screenplay. I don't know how to format it. I don't know how to structure the story. I don't even know the story I want to tell.

I'm afraid that I'll fail. That I'll spend a lot of time on it—while other more immediate things don't get done—and that it'll be terrible, anyway.

My screenplay is work I care about deeply. Almost all big projects fit into that category—including the competitive analysis your boss asked for. Because a big project is a mirror. Even if you think you don't care about it, a big project reflects your smarts, effort, and character. It has your signature on it. Failure in a long-term project isn't just a work issue, it's an identity issue.

So what's the antidote?

Acknowledge your fear

As soon as you know you're going to give that speech or design that training program, take a quiet moment and feel the fear that comes with the importance—and unknowns—of the project. Maybe you're afraid of getting in front of all those people to give your speech. Maybe you're afraid that your training design will expose how much you *don't* know. Maybe you're afraid of letting other people down.

Share your fear

Some people may think you're a wimp, but that hasn't been my experience. Telling others you're intimidated by something you have to do gives them permission to feel— and maybe express—their own fear. I find that people are gracious, supportive, and empathic.

Round up the tools you need

Acknowledging your fear also serves another, crucial purpose: it *informs* you. By recognizing that you don't have everything you need to see the project through, you're identifying your next, manageable step: gathering the necessary tools, information, skills, and support.

Lower your expectations

You're scared because you expect a lot from yourself and you're afraid you'll underperform. When you acknowledge that fear, you recognize that you might not have all that it takes to meet your expectations. Admitting that, in turn, reduces your expectation of getting it perfect right off the bat. And lowering your expectation of getting it right is key to getting started.

Make it a priority

Even if the long-term project isn't your choice—commit yourself to it fully. Make it one of your top five priorities. This forces you to also identify what's *not* a priority. If you have too many important goals, you'll never get to the big long-term ones. So slash your list until you're left with only five.

I use a six-box to-do list—each box represents one of my top five priorities and the sixth box, labeled "The Other 5%," is for everything else. (See figure 9-1, "Sample *18 Minutes* daily to-do list.") That last box shouldn't take more than 5% of your time. One of my five boxes always represents a long-term priority, which, for this year, contains my screenplay. Having a long-term project on my daily to-do list means every day I make incremental progress toward my big goal.

Break the work into smaller pieces, and set deadlines

Now you're ready for the standard advice. Break the work into manageable chunks and make sure you know how to do the first chunk. Set an intermediate deadline. If you need other people's help, get them involved early. Finally, decide when and where you're going to accomplish the

FIGURE 9-1

Sample *18 Minutes* daily to-do list

Date: _____

Do great work with current clients	Develop new business opportunities
- Follow-up meetings with Anycorp and Bigorg GMs - Mary appt for next week - Jason—on-boarding docs - Set up flight to SF - E-mail request to clients for Howie to call - Speak with Luisa about 360 Ideas for General Corporation leadership team	- Abigail—M&A work? - Referrals from Tom - Talk to Fernanda about real estate opportunity - Lunch with Joe
Speak and write about my ideas	**Express myself creatively**
- Next HBR article - Review changes to WSJ article - Speaking engagement call with Loretta - Rich—ideas for future management guides - Slides for keynote speech	- Talk with Alice about screenplay
Nurture myself and my family	**The other 5%**
- Write in journal 30 minutes/day - Type with Isabelle - Book flights to Bahamas - Exercise 60 minutes/day - Make reservation for dinner with Eleanor	- Dr. Clancy—confirm Wed CT scan - Call Tim - Lunch with Kathy to talk about job search - Andrew—Amex card - Research new running sneakers - Buy bathing suit - Get exact numbers from Kristin

first chunk and make an appointment with yourself in your calendar.

When you sit down to start your work, you may feel the resistance—fear—come up again. But now you know what it is. Acknowledge it, and it'll be easier to move into the work.

Peter Bregman is a strategic adviser to CEOs and their leadership teams. His latest book is *18 Minutes: Find Your Focus, Master Distraction, and Get the Right Things Done.*

Chapter 10
Stop Multitasking

by Peter Bregman

During a conference call with the executive committee of a nonprofit board on which I sit, I decided to send an e-mail to a client.

I know—multitasking is dangerous.

But I wasn't texting while driving. I was safe at my desk. What could go wrong?

Well, I sent the client the message. Then I had to send him another one, this time with the attachment I'd forgotten to append. Finally, my third e-mail to him explained why that attachment wasn't what he was expecting. When I eventually refocused on the call, I realized I hadn't heard a question the board's chair had asked me.

I swear I wasn't sleep-deprived or smoking anything. But I might as well have been. A study showed that people distracted by incoming e-mail and phone calls saw a 10-point drop in their IQs. What's the impact of

---

Adapted from content posted on hbr.org on May 20, 2009.

10 points? The same as losing a night of sleep. More than twice the effect of smoking marijuana.

Doing several things at once is a trick we play on ourselves, thinking we're getting more done. In reality, our productivity decreases by as much as 40%. We don't actually multitask. We switch-task, shifting rapidly from one thing to another, interrupting ourselves, and losing time in the process.

You might think you're different, that you've done it so much you've become good at it.

But research shows that heavy multitaskers are less competent at doing several things at once than light multitaskers. Unlike most things, the more you multitask, the worse you are at it. Practice, in this case, works against you.

I decided to try an experiment. For one week I would do no multitasking and see what happened. What techniques would help? Could I sustain a focus on one thing at a time for that long?

For the most part, I succeeded. If I was on the phone, I did nothing but participate in the conversation. In meetings, I was fully focused on the presentation or discussion at hand. And when I was working at my desk, I held off any interruptions—e-mail, a knock on the door—until I finished my task.

I discovered six things:

1. **It was delightful.** When I shut off my cell phone I was much more deeply engaged and present. While it may seem that thumbing out a text under the table during a meeting takes only a

split second, it's a longer distraction than that. First you think about your text, then you type it out, then you think about how the other person might respond, then you check for her response, etc. Before you know it, you've missed the whole meeting.

2. **I made significant progress on challenging projects.** Activities like writing or strategy work require thought and persistence. They're the kind I usually try to distract myself from. I stayed with each project when it got hard, and I experienced a number of breakthroughs.

3. **My stress level dropped dramatically.** Multitasking isn't just inefficient, it's stressful. It was a relief to focus on only one thing at a time. It felt reassuring to completely finish a task before moving to the next.

4. **I had no patience for wasted time.** I became laser-focused on getting things done. An hour-long meeting seemed interminable. A meandering conversation was excruciating.

5. **I had tremendous patience for useful and enjoyable things.** When I was on a call with a client, I closed my computer, shut my eyes, and focused completely. I was able to pick up nuance and subtle emotion. And when I was brainstorming about a difficult problem, I stuck with it. Nothing else was competing for my attention, so I was able to settle into the one thing I was doing.

6. **There was no downside.** I lost nothing by not multitasking. No projects were left unfinished. No one became frustrated with me for not answering a call or failing to return an e-mail the second I received it.

So how do we resist the temptation to multitask?

Turn off interruptions

Often I write at 6 AM, when there's nothing to distract me. I shut down my computer's wireless connection and turn off my phone. In my car, I leave my phone in the trunk. Drastic? Maybe. But most of us shouldn't trust ourselves.

Prioritize

Say you're the only person with information that your team needs in order to move forward with a time-sensitive project, but you're on an important conference call. What do you do? Decide which task is more important to focus on and ask the other one to wait. Making a conscious choice to interrupt one task for another is better than trying to do them at the same time. So either excuse yourself from the conference call for a moment, or tell your team to wait until you're done.

Use your loss of patience to your advantage

Create unrealistically short deadlines. Cut all meetings in half. Give yourself a third of the time you think you need to accomplish something.

There's nothing like a deadline to keep things moving. And when things are moving fast, we can't help but focus on them. If it turns out you only have 30 minutes to finish a presentation you thought would take an hour, are you really going to answer your cell phone?

Because multitasking is so stressful, single-tasking to meet a tight deadline will actually reduce your stress. And giving yourself less time to do things may make you even more productive and relaxed.

Peter Bregman is a strategic adviser to CEOs and their leadership teams. His latest book is *18 Minutes: Find Your Focus, Master Distraction, and Get the Right Things Done.*

Chapter 11
How to Stay Focused on What's Important

by Gina Trapani

Most of us spend our workdays in one of two ways: reacting to urgent demands, or proactively focusing on what we decided ahead of time are our most critical tasks to accomplish. The best way to be productive is to mitigate the urgent to work on the important.

What's the difference between urgent and important? "Urgent" tasks include things like:

- Frantic e-mails that need a response "right now"

- Sudden requests that seem like they'll take only two minutes but instead take an hour

Adapted from content posted on hbr.org on February 18, 2009.

- Putting out fires—especially others'

- Fixing the day's crisis rather than stepping back to consider what will solve the chronic problem

- Tasks you'd rather do first because they're less intimidating than your priorities

We're drawn to these seemingly "urgent" tasks because they keep us busy and make us feel needed and essential. If we label projects as urgent, it justifies the time and attention we throw at them.

But dealing with a constant stream of "urgent" tasks leaves you wrung out at the end of the day, wondering where all your time went, staring at the important work you've yet to start, much less complete.

On the flip side, important work:

- Moves you and your business toward long-term goals

- Can be hard work that feels scary because you're not confident you can actually do it

- May not give you that same shot of adrenaline that "urgent" requests do

If your workplace encourages constant, frantic headless-chicken running, it can feel impossible to focus on what's actually important versus what seems urgent. Still, an awareness of the difference and a few simple techniques can help. Here are three.

Choose three important tasks to complete each day

Write them down on a slip of paper and keep it visible on your desk. If, for example, you're tempted to respond to an e-mail notification, check your list and remember that that "ding" probably has nothing to do with your most critical work. When you have an unexpected hour thanks to a canceled meeting, move forward on those three important tasks.

Turn off your e-mail

Shut down Outlook, turn off e-mail notifications on your mobile, and do whatever else you have to do to muffle e-mail interruptions. When you decide to work on one of your important tasks, give yourself at least an hour of uninterrupted time to complete it. If the Web is too much of a temptation, disconnect your computer from the Internet for that hour.

Set up a weekly 20-minute meeting with yourself

Put it on your calendar, and don't book over it—treat it with the same respect you'd treat a meeting with your boss. If you don't have an office door or you work in a busy open area, book a conference room. Go there to be alone. Bring your project list, to-do list, and calendar, and spend the time reviewing what you finished in the past week and what you want to get done next week. This is a great time to choose your daily three important tasks. Productivity author David Allen refers to this as the "weekly review," and it's one of the most effective ways to be mindful of how you're spending your time.

For other ideas on how to tackle your day, see "Power Through Your Day in 90-Minute Cycles" (later in this guide) and "A Practical Plan for When You Feel Overwhelmed" (earlier in this guide).

———————

Gina Trapani is the founding editor of the personal productivity blog Lifehacker.com.

Chapter 12
To-Do Lists That Work

by Gina Trapani

Here's how to write to-do lists that work:

1. **Break it down.** Take a task and carve it into bite-sized chunks. Then break it down some more. Don't confuse to-do's with goals or projects. A to-do is a single, specific action that will move a project toward completion. It's just one step. For example, "Plan the committee lunch" is a project. "E-mail Karen to get catering contact" is a to-do.

   Breaking down your task into the smallest possible actions forces you to think through each step up front. With the thinking out of the way, it's easy to dash off that e-mail, make

---

Adapted from content posted on hbr.org on January 13, 2009.

that call, or file that report, and move your
work along with much less resistance.

2. **Use specific action verbs and include details**
You're overdue for a check-in with your mentor, but the "Lunch with Judy" to-do just
hasn't gotten done. When you write down
that task, use an action verb (call? e-mail?)
and include whatever details your future self
needs to check it off. "Call Judy at 555–4567
for lunch on January 17, 18, or 19" is a specific,
detailed to-do.

Make your to-do's small and specific to set yourself up for
that glorious moment when you can cross them off your
list as *DONE*.

Here are some more tips for effective to-do lists from
the hbr.org community.

- Bucket your work in any way that makes sense
  for you (for example, work/home/freelance); by
  area of responsibility (Smith account/Culver ac-
  count/web team); by difficulty level (group all of
  your "easy" five-minute tasks together so when
  you have spare time, you can quickly spot them
  and knock a few off). Give each bucket its own
  column.

- Deliberately use a small-trim book or paper
  (6″ × 9″) to keep your list short or a distinctive size
  (like an 8.5″ × 11″ piece of paper folded in half)
  that makes it stand out from other papers you
  carry.

- Make a two-view list. Two lists, with the same to-do's, but one organized by buckets, one by week. Bonus: You get the joy of crossing off one task in *TWO* places.

- Pick a medium that works for you: a notebook you love (for example, Moleskine); a web-based app that syncs on your mobile and computer, wherever you are; your mobile's voice-memo function.

- Make notes in the margin or beside an item to mark when it's due (M or 2/16).

- Highlight your top-priority items or put a bright-colored sticky with your top three things to do for the day on top of your longer list/buckets.

- Build in rewards. For example, for every three things you cross off your work list, allow yourself to do one home/personal task; or for every one difficult work task you accomplish, reward yourself with three easy or fun work ones.

- Rewrite your list every other day or so to help you reprioritize.

- When a task is done, check off a box or cross off the item with a fat marker—whatever gives you the most satisfaction.

———————

Gina Trapani is the founding editor of the personal productivity blog Lifehacker.com.

Chapter 13
How to Tackle Your To-Do List

by Peter Bregman

For many of us, our to-do list has become more of a guilt list: an inventory of everything we want to do and really should do, but never get to. And the longer the list, the less likely we'll get to everything on it, and the more stressed we become.

So how do we turn *intention* into *action*?

It's the power of when and where.

Decide when and where you'll do something, and the likelihood that you'll follow through increases dramatically. The reason we're always left with unfinished items on our to-do lists is because they're the wrong tool to drive our accomplishments. A list is useful as a *collection* tool—to ensure we know the pool of things that we need to do.

Adapted from content posted on hbr.org on March 2, 2011.

A calendar, on the other hand, is the perfect tool to guide our daily accomplishments. A calendar is finite; there are only so many available hours. This becomes clear the instant we try to cram an unrealistic number of things into any one day.

Once you have your to-do list, open your calendar and decide when and where you're going to do each item. Schedule each task for a specific time, placing the most challenging and important items at the beginning of the day—before even checking your e-mail.

Since your entire to-do list won't fit into your calendar, prioritize. What do you really need to do today? What important items have you been ignoring? Where can you slot them into your schedule? Once you schedule an item, cross it off your list.

Transferring items from your to-do list to your calendar will help you make strategic choices about where you spend your time, but it will also leave you with a long list of items that didn't fit into your calendar for the day.

What do you do with those things?

I created a three-day rule to prevent items from haunting me indefinitely.

Here's what I do: After I've filled my calendar for the day, I review what's left on the list. I leave new items, those I just added that day or in the previous two days, on the list to see if they make it onto my calendar the following day.

But for everything else—anything that's been on my calendar for three days—I do one of four things:

1. **Do it immediately.** I'm often amazed at how many things have been sitting on my list for

days that, when I finally decide to do them, take no time at all. Often they turn out to be 30-second voice mails or two-minute e-mails.

2. **Schedule it.** For those things that I don't do immediately, I look for a time to slot them into my calendar, even if it's six months away. If it's important enough for me to have on my list, then I need to commit to doing it at a specific time and day. I can always change my plan when I review my calendar for that day, but if I want to do it, I need to schedule it.

3. **Let it go.** That's a nice way of saying delete the to-do. If I'm not willing to do something immediately or schedule it for a specific time and day, I won't ever do it. I face the reality that while I might like these things to be priorities, they currently aren't.

4. **Add it to a someday/maybe list.** Sometimes it's too hard to delete something. I don't want to admit that I'm not going to do it. And I want to remember that I think, someday, maybe it would be a good idea. So I put those items in a someday/maybe list, which I learned about from David Allen, author of *Getting Things Done*. It's where I put things to slowly die. I rarely, if ever, do things on this list. I look at it occasionally, get rid of the items that are no longer relevant, and then put the list away for another month. I probably could delete everything on this list, but I sleep a little better

knowing I can put things on it when I'm not courageous or guilt-free enough to do away with them right off the bat. And who knows? Perhaps someday, maybe, I'll do something on that list.

Peter Bregman is a strategic adviser to CEOs and their leadership teams. His latest book is *18 Minutes: Find Your Focus, Master Distraction, and Get the Right Things Done.*

Chapter 14
Reward Yourself for Doing Dreaded Tasks

by Alexandra Samuel

For some of us, checking off each item on our to-do lists provides the endorphin rush we need to make task completion an intrinsic joy. But most of us need a little extra motivation, especially for boring work like recording billable hours, uncomfortable tasks like facing awkward conversations with dissatisfied clients, or major projects like writing a complex case study. Setting up a compelling reward system can help you power through your to-dos.

Here are some types of rewards to consider:

Regenerative

By rewarding yourself in a way that recharges your body and brain, you'll give yourself more energy to tackle your next task or project. Use these brief rewards midmorning, midafternoon, or midproject to help maintain your momentum. Examples of regenerative rewards include:

- Meditating for 20 minutes in a secluded spot

- Using your lunch hour to treat yourself to a yoga class, run, or walk

- Doing 5 to 10 minutes of stretches in your office, guided by a video on your computer or iPad

- Talking with a good friend for 5 or 10 minutes

- Treating yourself to a second cup of coffee or a snack after an hour of focused work

Productive

Often—hopefully—work is rewarding in and of itself: meeting with colleagues you respect and enjoy or crafting a PowerPoint deck that incorporates self-deprecating humor or favorite photographs. Use these aspects of your job as rewards for completing something more difficult or tedious. Other examples of productive rewards include:

- Reading a popular business book or article

- Taking a working meeting to a good restaurant

- Installing or tweaking a piece of software you've been eager to use

- Reading/posting an article you think your colleagues/clients would enjoy to Twitter, LinkedIn, or Google+

- Cleaning your desk

Concurrent

Some tasks are so odious or boring that even the prospect of a pint of ice cream can't help you face them. These tasks call for a concurrent reward: something you do *while* working so that you can bear to plow through your in-box backlog or complete your quarterly budget report.

This type of reward works especially well for tasks that are time-consuming but not concentration-intensive. You can make even difficult tasks that require your full concentration more pleasant in the right setting. Some concurrent rewards include:

- Setting up camp in a Wi-Fi-enabled restaurant so you can eat while you work

- Making a work date with a friend so you can chat while you purge your e-mail in-boxes

- Storing up mindless tasks to complete while watching your favorite TV show at home

- Downloading some new music to listen to while you purge your files

- Making arrangements to work from home for the day

Cumulative

Establish a special-purpose account to pay into every time you complete an especially challenging or large project. Set different dollar values depending on the size and unpleasantness of the task. Examples include:

- An iTunes account

- A replenishable gift card to your favorite coffee shop or store

- A PayPal account you can refill with quick micropayments to treat yourself to some online shopping

- A discretionary savings account that you use to fund something significant like tickets to a sports or arts event

You'll know your reward system is working when your to-do list no longer includes tasks you've been avoiding for weeks, or when you find yourself racing to complete your least-favorite work so that you can get to that delicious brownie, fantastic concert, or backlog of *Mad Men* episodes.

———————

Alexandra Samuel is the Director of the Social + Interactive Media Centre at Emily Carr University, and the cofounder of Social Signal, a Vancouver-based social media agency. You can follow Alex on Twitter at @awsamuel or her blog at alexandrasamuel.com.

Section 4
Delegate Effectively

Chapter 15
Management Time
Who's Got the Monkey?

A summary of the full-length HBR article by **William Oncken, Jr.,** *and* **Donald L. Wass,** *highlighting key ideas, with commentary by* **Stephen R. Covey.**

THE IDEA IN BRIEF

You're racing down the hall. An employee stops you and says, "We've got a problem." You assume you should get involved but can't make an on-the-spot decision. You say, "Let me think about it."

You've just allowed a "monkey" to leap from your employee's back to yours. You're now working for the person who works for you. Take on enough monkeys, and you won't have time to focus on your own priorities.

Reprint #99609

How do you avoid accumulating monkeys? Develop your employees' initiative. For example, when one of your people tries to hand you a problem, clarify whether he should: recommend and then implement a solution; take action, then brief you immediately; or act and report the outcome at a regular update.

When you encourage your employees to handle their own monkeys, they acquire new skills—and you gain time to do your own job.

THE IDEA IN PRACTICE

How do you return monkeys to their proper owners? Try these tactics:

Make Appointments to Deal with Monkeys

Avoid discussing any monkey on an ad hoc basis—for example, when you pass an employee in the hall. You won't convey the proper seriousness. Instead, have your employee schedule an appointment to discuss the issue.

Specify Level of Initiative

Your employees can exercise five levels of initiative in handling on-the-job problems. From lowest to highest, the levels are:

1. Wait until told what to do.

2. Ask what to do.

3. Recommend an action, then with your approval, implement it.

4. Take independent action but advise you at once.

5. Take independent action and update you at an agreed-on time; for example, your weekly meeting.

When an employee brings a problem to you, outlaw use of level 1 or 2. Agree on and assign level 3, 4, or 5 to the monkey. Take no more than 15 minutes to discuss the problem.

Agree on a Status Update

After deciding how to proceed, agree on a time and place when the employee will give you a progress report.

Develop Employees' Skills

Employees try to hand off monkeys when they lack the desire or ability to handle them. Help employees develop needed problem-solving skills. It's initially more time-consuming than tackling problems yourself—but it saves time in the long run.

Foster Trust

Developing employees' initiative requires a trusting relationship. If they're afraid of failing, they'll keep bringing their monkeys to you rather than working to solve their own problems. To promote trust, reassure them that it's safe to make mistakes.

Why is it that managers are typically running out of time while their subordinates are typically running out of work? Here we shall explore the meaning of management time as it relates to the interaction between managers and their bosses, their peers, and their subordinates.

Specifically, we shall deal with three kinds of management time:

Boss-imposed time—used to accomplish those activities that the boss requires and that the manager cannot disregard without direct and swift penalty.

System-imposed time—used to accommodate requests from peers for active support. Neglecting these requests will also result in penalties, though not always as direct or swift.

Self-imposed time—used to do those things that the manager originates or agrees to do. A certain portion of this kind of time, however, will be taken by subordinates and is called subordinate-imposed time. The remaining portion will be the manager's own and is called discretionary time. Self-imposed time is not subject to penalty since neither the boss nor the system can discipline the manager for not doing what they didn't know he had intended to do in the first place.

To accommodate those demands, managers need to control the timing and the content of what they do. Since what their bosses and the system impose on them are subject to penalty, managers cannot tamper with those requirements. Thus their self-imposed time becomes their major area of concern.

Managers should try to increase the discretionary component of their self-imposed time by minimizing or doing away with the subordinate component. They will then use the added increment to get better control over their boss-imposed and system-imposed activities. Most managers spend much more time dealing with subordinates' problems than they even faintly realize. Hence we shall use the monkey-on-the-back metaphor to examine how subordinate-imposed time comes into being and what the superior can do about it.

Where Is the Monkey?

Let us imagine that a manager is walking down the hall and that he notices one of his subordinates, Jones, coming his way. When the two meet, Jones greets the manager with, "Good morning. By the way, we've got a problem. You see . . . ." As Jones continues, the manager recognizes in this problem the two characteristics common to all the problems his subordinates gratuitously bring to his attention. Namely, the manager knows (a) enough to get involved, but (b) not enough to make the on-the-spot decision expected of him. Eventually, the manager says, "So glad you brought this up. I'm in a rush right now. Meanwhile, let me think about it, and I'll let you know." Then he and Jones part company.

Let us analyze what just happened. Before the two of them met, on whose back was the "monkey"? The subordinate's. After they parted, on whose back was it? The manager's. Subordinate-imposed time begins the moment a monkey successfully leaps from the back of a subordinate to the back of his or her superior and does not end until the monkey is returned to its proper owner for care and feeding. In accepting the monkey, the manager has voluntarily assumed a position subordinate to his subordinate. That is, he has allowed Jones to make him her subordinate by doing two things a subordinate is generally expected to do for a boss—the manager has accepted a responsibility from his subordinate, and the manager has promised her a progress report.

The subordinate, to make sure the manager does not miss this point, will later stick her head in the manager's office and cheerily query, "How's it coming?" (This is called supervision.)

Or let us imagine in concluding a conference with Johnson, another subordinate, the manager's parting words are, "Fine. Send me a memo on that."

Let us analyze this one. The monkey is now on the subordinate's back because the next move is his, but it is poised for a leap. Watch that monkey. Johnson dutifully writes the requested memo and drops it in his out-basket. Shortly thereafter, the manager plucks it from his in-basket and reads it. Whose move is it now? The manager's. If he does not make that move soon, he will get a follow-up memo from the subordinate. (This is another form of supervision.) The longer the manager delays, the more frustrated the subordinate will become (he'll be spinning his wheels) and the more guilty the manager will feel (his backlog of subordinate-imposed time will be mounting).

Or suppose once again that at a meeting with a third subordinate, Smith, the manager agrees to provide all the necessary backing for a public relations proposal he has just asked Smith to develop. The manager's parting words to her are, "Just let me know how I can help."

Now let us analyze this. Again the monkey is initially on the subordinate's back. But for how long? Smith realizes that she cannot let the manager "know" until her proposal has the manager's approval. And from experience, she also realizes that her proposal will likely be sitting in the manager's briefcase for weeks before he eventually gets to it. Who's really got the monkey? Who will be checking up on whom? Wheel spinning and bottlenecking are well on their way again.

A fourth subordinate, Reed, has just been transferred from another part of the company so that he can launch and eventually manage a newly created business venture. The manager has said they should get together soon to hammer out a set of objectives for the new job, adding, "I will draw up an initial draft for discussion with you."

Let us analyze this one, too. The subordinate has the new job (by formal assignment) and the full responsibility (by formal delegation), but the manager has the next move. Until he makes it, he will have the monkey, and the subordinate will be immobilized.

Why does all of this happen? Because in each instance the manager and the subordinate assume at the outset, wittingly or unwittingly, that the matter under consideration is a joint problem. The monkey in each case begins its career astride both their backs. All it has to do is

MAKING TIME FOR GORILLAS

by Stephen R. Covey

When Bill Oncken wrote this article in 1974, managers were in a terrible bind. They were desperate for a way to free up their time, but command and control was the status quo. Managers felt they weren't allowed to empower their subordinates to make decisions. Too dangerous. Too risky. That's why Oncken's message—give the monkey back to its rightful owner—involved a critically important paradigm shift. Many managers working today owe him a debt of gratitude.

It is something of an understatement, however, to observe that much has changed since Oncken's radical recommendation. Command and control as a management philosophy is all but dead, and "empowerment" is the word of the day in most organizations trying to thrive in global, intensely competitive markets. But command and control stubbornly remains a common practice. Management thinkers and executives have discovered in the last decade that bosses cannot just give a monkey back to their subordinates and then merrily get on with their own business. Empowering subordinates is hard and complicated work.

The reason: when you give problems back to subordinates to solve themselves, you have to be sure that they have both the desire and the ability to do so. As every executive knows, that isn't always the case. Enter a whole new set of problems. Empowerment often means you have to develop people, which is initially much more time consuming than solving the problem on your own.

Just as important, empowerment can only thrive when the whole organization buys into it—when formal systems and the informal culture support it. Managers need to be rewarded for delegating decisions and developing people. Otherwise, the degree of real empowerment in an organization will vary according to the beliefs and practices of individual managers.

But perhaps the most important lesson about empowerment is that effective delegation—the kind Oncken advocated—depends on a trusting relationship between a manager and his subordinate. Oncken's message may have been ahead of his time, but what he suggested was still a fairly dictatorial solution. He basically told bosses, "Give the problem back!" Today, we know that this approach by itself is too authoritarian. To delegate effectively, executives need to establish a running dialogue with subordinates. They need to establish a partnership. After all, if subordinates are afraid of failing in front of their boss, they'll keep coming back for help rather than truly take initiative.

Oncken's article also doesn't address an aspect of delegation that has greatly interested me during the past two decades—that many managers are actually *eager* to take on their subordinates' monkeys. Nearly all the managers I talk with agree that their people are underutilized in their present jobs. But even some of the most success-

(continued)

(continued)

ful, seemingly self-assured executives have talked about how hard it is to give up control to their subordinates.

I've come to attribute that eagerness for control to a common, deep-seated belief that rewards in life are scarce and fragile. Whether they learn it from their family, school, or athletics, many people establish an identity by comparing themselves with others. When they see others gain power, information, money, or recognition, for instance, they experience what the psychologist Abraham Maslow called "a feeling of deficiency"—a sense that something is being taken from them. That makes it hard for them to be genuinely happy about the success of others—even of their loved ones. Oncken implies that managers can easily give back or refuse monkeys, but many managers may subconsciously fear that a subordinate taking the initiative will make them appear a little less strong and a little more vulnerable.

How, then, do managers develop the inward security, the mentality of "abundance," that would enable them to relinquish control and seek the growth and development of those around them? The work I've done with numerous organizations suggests that managers who live with integrity according to a principle-based value system are most likely to sustain an empowering style of leadership.

Given the times in which he wrote, it was no wonder that Oncken's message resonated with managers. But it was reinforced by Oncken's wonderful gift for storytelling. I got to know Oncken on the speaker's circuit in the 1970s, and I was always impressed by how he dramatized his ideas in colorful detail. Like the Dilbert comic strip, Oncken had a tongue-in-cheek style that got to the core of managers' frustrations and made them want to take back control of their time. And the monkey on your back wasn't just a metaphor for Oncken—it was his personal symbol. I saw him several times walking through airports with a stuffed monkey on his shoulder.

I'm not surprised that his article is one of the two best-selling HBR articles ever. Even with all we know about empowerment, its vivid message is even more important and relevant now than it was 25 years ago. Indeed, Oncken's insight is a basis for my own work on time management, in which I have people categorize their activities according to urgency and importance. I've heard from executives again and again that half or more of their time is spent on matters that are urgent but not important. They're trapped in an endless cycle of dealing with other people's monkeys, yet they're reluctant to help those people take their own initiative. As a result, they're often too busy to spend the time they need on the real gorillas in their organization. Oncken's article remains a powerful wake-up call for managers who need to delegate effectively.

Stephen R. Covey is vice chairman of the Franklin Covey Company, a global provider of leadership development and productivity services and products. He is the author of *The 7 Habits of Highly Effective People* (Simon & Schuster, 1989) and *First Things First* (Simon & Schuster, 1994).

move the wrong leg, and—presto!—the subordinate deftly disappears.

The manager is thus left with another acquisition for his menagerie. Of course, monkeys can be trained not to move the wrong leg. But it is easier to prevent them from straddling backs in the first place.

Who Is Working for Whom?

Let us suppose that these same four subordinates are so thoughtful and considerate of their superior's time that they take pains to allow no more than three monkeys to leap from each of their backs to his in any one day. In a five-day week, the manager will have picked up 60 screaming monkeys—far too many to do anything about them individually. So he spends his subordinate-imposed time juggling his "priorities."

Late Friday afternoon, the manager is in his office with the door closed for privacy so he can contemplate the situation, while his subordinates are waiting outside to get their last chance before the weekend to remind him that he will have to "fish or cut bait." Imagine what they are saying to one another about the manager as they wait: "What a bottleneck. He just can't make up his mind. How anyone ever got that high up in our company without being able to make a decision we'll never know."

Worst of all, the reason the manager cannot make any of these "next moves" is that his time is almost entirely eaten up by meeting his own boss-imposed and system-imposed requirements. To control those tasks, he needs discretionary time that is in turn denied him when he is preoccupied with all these monkeys. The manager is caught in a vicious circle. But time is a-wasting (an understatement). The manager calls his secretary on the intercom and instructs her to tell his subordinates that he won't be able to see them until Monday morning. At 7 PM, he drives home, intending with firm resolve to return to the office tomorrow to get caught up over the weekend. He returns bright and early the next day only to see, on the nearest green of the golf course across from his office window, a foursome. Guess who?

That does it. He now knows who is really working for whom. Moreover, he now sees that if he actually accomplishes during this weekend what he came to accomplish, his subordinates' morale will go up so sharply that they will each raise the limit on the number of monkeys they will let jump from their backs to his. In short, he now sees, with the clarity of a revelation on a mountaintop, that the more he gets caught up, the more he will fall behind.

He leaves the office with the speed of a person running away from a plague. His plan? To get caught up on something else he hasn't had time for in years: a weekend with his family. (This is one of the many varieties of discretionary time.)

Sunday night he enjoys ten hours of sweet, untroubled slumber, because he has clear-cut plans for Monday. He is going to get rid of his subordinate-imposed time. In exchange, he will get an equal amount of discretionary time, part of which he will spend with his subordinates to make sure that they learn the difficult but rewarding managerial art called "The Care and Feeding of Monkeys."

The manager will also have plenty of discretionary time left over for getting control of the timing and the content not only of his boss-imposed time but also of his system-imposed time. It may take months, but compared with the way things have been, the rewards will be enormous. His ultimate objective is to manage his time.

Getting Rid of the Monkeys

The manager returns to the office Monday morning just late enough so that his four subordinates have collected outside his office waiting to see him about their monkeys. He calls them in one by one. The purpose of each interview is to take a monkey, place it on the desk between them, and figure out together how the next move might conceivably be the subordinate's. For certain monkeys, that will take some doing. The subordinate's next move may be so elusive that the manager may decide—just for now—merely to let the monkey sleep on the subordinate's back overnight and have him or her return with it at an appointed time the next morning to continue the joint quest for a more substantive move by the subordinate. (Monkeys sleep just as soundly overnight on subordinates' backs as they do on superiors'.)

As each subordinate leaves the office, the manager is rewarded by the sight of a monkey leaving his office on the subordinate's back. For the next 24 hours, the subordinate will not be waiting for the manager; instead, the manager will be waiting for the subordinate.

Later, as if to remind himself that there is no law against his engaging in a constructive exercise in the interim, the manager strolls by the subordinate's office, sticks his head in the door, and cheerily asks, "How's it coming?" (The time consumed in doing this is discretionary for the manager and boss imposed for the subordinate.)

When the subordinate (with the monkey on his or her back) and the manager meet at the appointed hour the next day, the manager explains the ground rules in words to this effect:

> *At no time while I am helping you with this or any other problem will your problem become my problem. The instant your problem becomes mine, you no longer have a problem. I cannot help a person who hasn't got a problem.*
>
> *When this meeting is over, the problem will leave this office exactly the way it came in—on your back. You may ask my help at any appointed time, and we will make a joint determination of what the next move will be and which of us will make it.*
>
> *In those rare instances where the next move turns out to be mine, you and I will determine it together. I will not make any move alone.*

The manager follows this same line of thought with each subordinate until about 11 AM, when he realizes that he doesn't have to close his door. His monkeys are gone. They will return—but by appointment only. His calendar will assure this.

Transferring the Initiative

What we have been driving at in this monkey-on-the-back analogy is that managers can transfer initiative back

THE DELEGATION CHECKLIST

by Peter Bregman

When it comes to delegating effectively, communication is key. Most of us think we communicate well, which is why we often inadvertently leave out important information. Sometimes we assume that the people to whom we're delegating share our understanding. Or we resist clarifying something because we don't want to insult the person.

Thankfully, there's a simple solution to ensure projects you delegate will transfer well: Create a checklist and use it during every handoff.

Before you pass off a project, complete the delegation checklist with the person who'll be taking on the responsibility. Reviewing the list together ensures that you transfer all important information. With the following questions as a starting point, add or delete some to suit your particular situation. It takes no longer than 10 minutes to complete the checklist, but it could save you countless dropped balls and service failures.

to their subordinates and keep it there. We have tried to highlight a truism as obvious as it is subtle: namely, before developing initiative in subordinates, the manager must see to it that they *have* the initiative. Once the manager takes it back, he will no longer have it and he can kiss his discretionary time good-bye. It will all revert to subordinate-imposed time.

Delegation Checklist

- What do you understand the priorities of this project to be?

- What are your next key steps, and by when do you plan to accomplish them?

- What key contingencies should you plan for now?

- When will you next check in with me on progress/issues?

- Who else needs to know our plans, and how will you communicate them?

- What concerns or ideas do you have that we haven't already discussed?

Adapted from content posted on hbr.org on January 25, 2011.
Peter Bregman is a strategic adviser to CEOs and their leadership teams. His latest book is *10 Minutes: Find Your Focus, Master Distraction, and Get the Right Things Done.*

Nor can the manager and the subordinate effectively have the same initiative at the same time. The opener, "Boss, we've got a problem," implies this duality and represents, as noted earlier, a monkey astride two backs, which is a very bad way to start a monkey on its career. Let us, therefore, take a few moments to examine what we call "The Anatomy of Managerial Initiative."

There are five degrees of initiative that the manager can exercise in relation to the boss and to the system:

1. wait until told (lowest initiative);

2. ask what to do;

3. recommend, then take resulting action;

4. act, but advise at once;

5. and act on own, then routinely report (highest initiative).

Clearly, the manager should be professional enough not to indulge in initiatives 1 and 2 in relation either to

TIPS FOR DELEGATING EFFECTIVELY

- Recognize the capabilities of your employees and trust their ability to get the job done.

- Consider delegation a development opportunity—a way to broaden your people's skills.

- Focus on results and let go of your need to get involved in *how* tasks are accomplished.

- Explain assignments clearly and provide resources needed for successful completion.

- Always delegate to the lowest possible level to make the best use of staff resources.

Adapted from *Pocket Mentor: Managing Projects* (product #1878), Harvard Business Review Press, 2006.

the boss or to the system. A manager who uses initiative 1 has no control over either the timing or the content of boss-imposed or system-imposed time and thereby forfeits any right to complain about what he or she is told to do or when. The manager who uses initiative 2 has control over the timing but not over the content. Initiatives 3, 4, and 5 leave the manager in control of both, with the greatest amount of control being exercised at level 5.

In relation to subordinates, the manager's job is twofold. First, to outlaw the use of initiatives 1 and 2, thus giving subordinates no choice but to learn and master "Completed Staff Work." Second, to see that for each problem leaving his or her office there is an agreed-upon level of initiative assigned to it, in addition to an agreed-upon time and place for the next manager-subordinate conference. The latter should be duly noted on the manager's calendar.

The Care and Feeding of Monkeys

To further clarify our analogy between the monkey on the back and the processes of assigning and controlling, we shall refer briefly to the manager's appointment schedule, which calls for five hard-and-fast rules governing the "Care and Feeding of Monkeys." (Violation of these rules will cost discretionary time.)

Rule 1

Monkeys should be fed or shot. Otherwise, they will starve to death, and the manager will waste valuable time on postmortems or attempted resurrections.

Rule 2

The monkey population should be kept below the maximum number the manager has time to feed. Subordinates will find time to work as many monkeys as he or she finds time to feed, but no more. It shouldn't take more than five to 15 minutes to feed a properly maintained monkey.

Rule 3

Monkeys should be fed by appointment only. The manager should not have to hunt down starving monkeys and feed them on a catch-as-catch-can basis.

Rule 4

Monkeys should be fed face to face or by telephone, but never by mail. (Remember—with mail, the next move will be the manager's.) Documentation may add to the feeding process, but it cannot take the place of feeding.

Rule 5

Every monkey should have an assigned next feeding time and degree of initiative. These may be revised at any time by mutual consent but never allowed to become vague or indefinite. Otherwise, the monkey will either starve to death or wind up on the manager's back.

"Get control over the timing and content of what you do" is appropriate advice for managing time. The first order of business is for the manager to enlarge his or her discretionary time by eliminating subordinate-imposed time.

The second is for the manager to use a portion of this newfound discretionary time to see to it that each subordinate actually has the initiative and applies it. The third is for the manager to use another portion of the increased discretionary time to get and keep control of the timing and content of both boss-imposed and system-imposed time. All these steps will increase the manager's leverage and enable the value of each hour spent in managing management time to multiply without theoretical limit.

William Oncken, Jr., was chairman of the William Oncken Corporation until his death in 1988. His son, William Oncken III, now heads the company. **Donald L. Wass** was president of the William Oncken Company of Texas when the article first appeared. He now heads the Dallas–Fort Worth region of The Executive Committee (TEC), an international organization for presidents and CEOs.

Chapter 16
Levels of Delegation

by Linda A. Hill and Kent Lineback

If you think that delegation is appropriate only for employees who've already demonstrated complete competence in an area, then you may be trapped in this vicious cycle: Until your employee has the opportunity to perform an activity by herself, she'll never develop the necessary skill and experience to do it well. But until she does it well, you'll continue to believe that you must be involved—either by performing the task yourself or by micromanaging her so closely she never learns to do it independently.

Here's a way to think about delegation as three levels corresponding to your direct reports' increasing levels of competence:

Delegation level 1 Low delegation—high control	Delegation level 2 Moderate delegation—moderate control	Delegation level 3 High delegation—low control
Use with someone about to do work he's never or rarely done before	**Use with** someone who has some experience, perhaps someone who's observed others and should be ready to act on her own	**Use with** someone who has actually demonstrated competence
Prep: Here the problem is more likely one of skill versus will, so describe how to do the work and coach him through the steps involved. Make clear the boundaries: budget, strategy, policy, and so on. If appropriate, take him through practice runs. If the problem is also one of will, set the activity in the context of the team's work and its purpose and goals. Make sure he understands the consequences of possible outcomes.	**Prep:** Ask her to describe her plan for doing the work and the various "What . . . ?" questions. Satisfy yourself that she's well prepared and ready. Explain constraints or boundaries. Agree on what constitutes success. Coach as necessary. Make sure she understands the reason for doing the work and why it's important. See whether she can link to team purpose and goals.	**Prep:** Leave the prep to him. Involve yourself only if the work—say, a discussion he will have with an important prospective customer—is unusually important to team purpose and goals. If it is, ask for his preparatory thinking. Provide clear direction and boundaries. Agree on success. Here the issue may be more one of will than skill, so make sure he understands the importance and consequences of the action.
Do: At first, you do the work as he observes. If the consequences of failure are low, you could observe while he performs the task.	**Do:** Let her do the work, perhaps with you present observing, perhaps alone, depending on the situation and your judgment of her readiness.	**Do:** He conducts the discussion without your involvement or presence.
Review: Walk through what you (or he) did. Answer questions. Identify lessons. Have him describe how he would do it next time.	**Review:** Ask for her self-assessment of how it went, in terms of both skill and will. What went well and what could be improved? Then, if you were present, give your assessment and discuss any differences. Identify lessons. Focus on tangible outcomes and specific behaviors. If you couldn't be present, ask others who were there. Reach agreement with her about what should be different or better next time.	**Review:** If this was routine work and it had a good or expected outcome, you won't have a review discussion except as part of a periodic general performance review. If it was more than routine work or the outcome was unexpected, ask for his self-assessment of what happened and what might be learned from it.

Source: Reprinted with permission from *Being the Boss: The 3 Imperatives for Becoming a Great Leader* by Linda A. Hill and Kent Lineback. Harvard Business Review Press, 2011.

Section 5
Create Rituals

Chapter 17
Ritual

How to Get Important Work Done

by Tony Schwartz

Most of us feel pulled in more directions than ever, expected to work longer hours, and asked to get more done, often with fewer resources. But we also know people who get lots done, including the important stuff, and still manage to have lives.

What have they figured out that the rest of us haven't?

The answer, surprisingly, isn't that they have more will or discipline than we do. The counterintuitive secret to getting things done is to make them more automatic, so they require less energy.

How do we do that? By developing **rituals—highly specific behaviors, done at precise times, so they**

Adapted from content posted on hbr.org on May 24, 2011.

eventually become automatic and no longer require conscious will or discipline. Decide what behavior you want to change, design the ritual you'll undertake, and then get out of your own way.

Over the past decade, I've built a series of rituals into my daily schedule to make sure that I get to the most important things—and that I don't get derailed by the endlessly alluring trivia of everyday life.

Here are four of the rituals that have made the biggest difference to me:

1. **Going to bed at the same time every night.** This ritual ensures that I get eight hours of sleep. Nothing is more critical to the way I feel every day. If I'm flying somewhere and know I'll arrive too late to get my eight hours, I make it a priority to make up the hours I need on the plane.

2. **Working out as soon as I wake up.** Since exercise has a huge impact on how I feel all day long, this ritual ensures that I work out even when I don't feel like it.

3. **Launching my workday by focusing first on whatever I've decided the night before is my most important activity.** Then I take a break after 90 minutes to refuel. Today—which happens to be a Sunday—this blog was my priority. My break was playing tennis for an hour. During the week it might be chatting with a colleague for a few minutes or getting a snack. (Working

in 90-minute segments throughout your day can be another useful ritual to develop. See the next article, "Power Through Your Day in 90-Minute Cycles," to learn more.)

4. **Immediately writing down on a list any idea or task that occurs to me over the course of the day.** Once it's on paper, it means I don't walk around feeling preoccupied by it—or risk forgetting it.

Obviously, I'm human and fallible, so I don't perform every one of these rituals every day. But when I do miss one, I pay the price, and feel even more pulled to it the next day.

Tony Schwartz is the president and CEO of The Energy Project and the author of *Be Excellent at Anything.* Become a fan of The Energy Project and connect with Tony on Twitter at @tonyschwartz and @energy_project.

Chapter 18
Power Through Your Day in 90-Minute Cycles

by Tony Schwartz

For nearly a decade, I've begun my workdays by focusing for 90 minutes, uninterrupted, on the task I decide the night before is the most important to tackle the following day. After 90 minutes, I take a break. When my break is up, I begin the cycle again.

To make this possible, I turn off my e-mail while I'm working, close unnecessary windows on my computer, and let the phone go to voice mail.

I typically get more work done and feel more satisfied than I do for any comparable period of time the rest of the day. It can be tough on some days to fully focus

---

Adapted from content posted on hbr.org on May 24, 2011.

for 90 minutes, but I always have a clear stopping time, which makes it easier.

I launched this practice because my energy, will, and capacity for intense focus diminish as the day wears on. Anything really challenging that I put off tends not to get done, and it's the most difficult work that generally produces the greatest value. Usually, that means a challenge that is "important but not urgent," to use Steven Covey's language. These are precisely the types of activities we most often postpone in favor of those that are more urgent, easier to accomplish, or provide more immediate gratification. (See "How to Stay Focused on What's Important," earlier in this guide.)

I first made this discovery while writing a book. At the time, I'd written three previous books. For each one, I'd dutifully sit down at my desk at 7 AM and I'd often stay there until 7 PM.

I never finished a book in less than a year. Looking back, I probably spent more time avoiding writing than I did actually writing. I made lists, responded to e-mail, answered the phone, and kept my desk clean and my files well organized. There were days I never got to writing at all. It was incredibly frustrating.

For my new book, *The Way We're Working Isn't Working*, I wrote without interruptions for three 90-minute periods and took a break between each one. I had breakfast after the first session, went for a run after the second, and had lunch after the third. I wrote no more than 4 ½ hours a day, and finished the book in fewer than six months. By writing in several cycles of 90 minutes each and building in periods of renewal, I was able to focus far more intensely and get more done in less time.

What made me so productive? Creating the ritual of tackling the most important work at the start of the day and working with my body's natural rhythms. At the heart of making this work is to build highly precise, deliberate rituals, done at specific times, so they eventually become automatic and don't require much expenditure of energy or self-discipline, akin to brushing your teeth at night.

Pioneering sleep researcher Nathaniel Kleitman observed that our bodies operate by the same 90-minute "basic rest-activity" cycle during the day that we do when we sleep. When we're awake, we move from higher to lower alertness every 90 minutes. This "ultradian rhythm," researcher Peretz Lavie and others have found, governs our energy levels. The human body is hardwired to pulse, and requires renewal at regular intervals, not just physically, but also mentally and emotionally.

Many of us unwittingly train ourselves to ignore signals from our body that we need a rest—difficulty concentrating, physical restlessness, irritability. Instead, we find ways to override this need with caffeine, sugar, and our own stress hormones—adrenalin, noradrenalin, and cortisol—all of which provide short bursts of energy but impair our ability to consistently focus on our work for a significant period of time.

By intentionally aligning with my body's natural rhythms, I've learned to listen to its signals. When I notice them, it usually means I've hit the 90-minute mark.

At that point, I take a break, even if I'm on a roll, because I've learned that if I don't, I'll pay the price later in the day.

When I'm not working on a book, I still choose the next day's most important work the night before, because I don't want to squander energy thinking about what to do during the time I've set aside to actually work. I start at a very specific time, because when I don't, I give myself license to procrastinate.

Ideally you'll be able to divide up your day into several 90-minute focused work segments, with brief periods of renewal in between each. However, it's not always possible to structure your days this way. So make it a high priority to find at least one time a day to focus single-mindedly on your most challenging and important task.

Tony Schwartz is the president and CEO of The Energy Project and the author of *Be Excellent at Anything*. Become a fan of The Energy Project on Facebook and connect with Tony on Twitter at @tonyschwartz and @energy_project.

Chapter 19
An 18-Minute Plan for Managing Your Day

by Peter Bregman

I began my day yesterday with the best intentions. I walked into my office in the morning with a vague sense of what I wanted to accomplish. Then I sat down, turned on my computer, and checked my e-mail. Two hours later, after fighting several fires, solving other people's problems, and dealing with whatever happened to be thrown at me through my computer and phone, I could hardly remember what I had originally set out to do.

Most of us start every day knowing we're not going to get it all done. So how we spend our time is a key strategic decision. That's why it's a good idea to create both a to-do list and a *to-don't* list.

But even with those lists, the challenge—as always—is execution. How can you stick to a plan when so many things threaten to derail it? How can you focus on just a few important tasks when so many others require your attention?

We need a trick.

Jack LaLanne, the fitness guru, knew all about tricks. He had one trick that I believe was his real secret power.

Ritual.

At the age of 94, he still spent the first two hours of his day exercising. Ninety minutes lifting weights and 30 minutes swimming or walking. Every morning. He needed to do so to achieve his goals: on his 95th birthday he planned to swim from the coast of California to Santa Catalina Island—a distance of 20 miles.

So he worked consistently and deliberately. He did the same things day in and day out. He cared about his fitness and he built it into his schedule.

Managing our time needs to become a ritual, too. Not simply a list or a vague sense of our priorities. That's not consistent or deliberate. It needs to be an ongoing process we follow, no matter what, to keep us focused on our priorities throughout the day.

We can do it in three steps that take fewer than 18 minutes over an eight-hour workday:

1. **(5 minutes): Set Your Plan for the Day.** Before turning on your computer, sit down with a blank piece of paper and decide what will make this day highly successful. What can you real-

istically accomplish that will further your goals and allow you to leave at the end of the day feeling productive? Write those things down. Now, most important, take your calendar and schedule those things into time slots, placing the hardest and most important items at the beginning of the day—before checking your e-mail. If your entire list doesn't fit into your calendar, reprioritize your list. There is tremendous power in deciding when you're going to do something. (See "How to Tackle Your To-Do List," earlier in this guide.)

2. **(1 minute every hour): Refocus.** Set your watch, phone, or computer to ring every hour. When it rings, take a deep breath, look at your list, and ask yourself: *Am I doing what I most need to be doing right now?* Then look at your calendar and deliberately recommit to how you're going to use the next hour. Manage your day hour by hour. Don't let the hours—or the inevitable interruptions—manage you.

3. **(5 minutes at end of day): Review.** Shut off your computer and review your day. What worked? Where did you focus? Where did you get distracted? What did you learn that will help you be more productive tomorrow?

The power of rituals is their predictability: You do the same thing in the same way over and over again. And the outcome of a ritual is predictable, too. If you choose your focus deliberately and wisely and consistently remind yourself of that focus, you will *stay* focused.

This particular ritual may not help you swim 20 miles through the ocean or live to be 100. But it may just help you leave your office feeling productive and successful. And, at the end of the day, isn't that a higher priority?

Peter Bregman is a strategic adviser to CEOs and their leadership teams. His latest book is *18 Minutes: Find Your Focus, Master Distraction, and Get the Right Things Done.*

Chapter 20
Use a 10-Minute Diary to Stay on Track

by Teresa Amabile and Steven Kramer

What's the best way to use the last 10 minutes of your day? Many productivity gurus recommend an end-of-the-day meeting with yourself to review your to-do list, check how you're doing against short- and long-term goals, or select the most challenging project you'll tackle the following day. Our research suggests that not only should you do an end-of-day review, but you'll reap the greatest benefits for your productivity and personal well-being if you actually record your thoughts in a "mini-diary." A work diary will improve your focus, track your progress, and make you more satisfied with your work—which will help you be even more productive.

No question: This reflective time is often the first thing that we drop when we're feeling overloaded. Adding a daily writing assignment—the word "diary" conjures up a long-term commitment—seems counterproductive to making headway on "real" work. So **try it for just one month,** focusing on just one short-term project (for example, developing a departmental staffing plan), or just one area of professional development (improving your presentation skills).

Take 10 minutes at the end of each workday, write no more than 100 words, and see what you've learned after four weeks. You may be surprised.

You'll get five benefits from keeping a work diary. You:

1. **Track your progress.** The diary is a record of your "small wins," incremental steps toward meaningful goals, that can boost your motivation—if only you take a moment to reflect on them.

2. **Plan.** You use the diary as a tool for drafting your next steps.

3. **Fuel personal growth.** The diary gives you a way of working through your difficult—even traumatic—events, gaining new perspectives on them.

4. **Sharpen your focus.** You identify your strengths, passions, and challenges by looking at patterns in your entries over time. For example, your diary may reveal that you've been spending a lot of time on low-priority issues. Reviewing your diary and identifying

this pattern can help you recommit to focusing your time and energy on your most important work.

5. **Develop patience.** The diary serves as a reminder during frustrating days that, in the past, you've persevered through days that, at the time, seemed even worse.

Our research shows that, of all these benefits, using a work diary to track your progress may be the most important one for your productivity and psychological well-being. As part of a massive study on the psychology of everyday work life, we collected nearly 12,000 diary entries from 238 professionals working on complex, creative projects. Our analyses revealed a big surprise. Of all the things that could make people feel both happy and highly motivated to dig into their work, the single most important event was simply making progress in work they cared about. We call this *the progress principle*, and it applies even when the progress is an incremental small win. When we see we're making progress, we're motivated to keep going, and it's easier to keep our focus—even when we encounter setbacks. Witness this example, from the diary of a software engineer in our study:

Today, when I started work [. . .] there was a note from a user regarding some work I had done for him. It was very complimentary and it made me feel pretty good. Also in the note was a request to go ahead with an enhancement to the database analysis package. I was able to code and load this request today in less than the estimated time, which makes me feel good. And I know it will please our user when he comes in tomorrow.

That entry probably took fewer than five minutes to write. Yet, at the end of the day, that engineer was quite happy—and seems motivated toward high productivity the next day, too. Making progress, and noting it, can provide a real lift—and give you the boost you need to keep working on the projects that will yield the greatest benefit for your organization and its customers.

Daily writing and review helps in negative situations, too. In the following entry, an employee struggles to gain a sense of control during a traumatic event in her company—a downsizing. Even though her own job might still be in jeopardy, her work diary helps her shape a healthy perspective; it enables her to focus on her work, amid swirling gossip and uncertainty. Her personal growth is almost palpable in this entry:

This morning, my project manager came over and sat next to me and asked me if I was okay after all the layoffs that went on yesterday. I thought that was really nice. We all had a very rough day yesterday, but I feel better today. In 45 days, we will all know our fate, and then we can get on with our lives one way or the other. The outcome of all this is really out of our control. I'm trying to concentrate on what IS in my control, by doing my job.

And here, in his final entry for our study, a professional tells us directly how valuable it was for him to fill out the diary questionnaire that we sent every day during his project:

> *I did find value in doing the questionnaires, especially when I was disciplined enough to do them at the end of the day, when everything was still fresh in my mind. It helped me to reflect on the day, my accomplishments, the team's work, and how I was feeling in general. When you're working at a hectic pace, reflection time is rare, but [it's] really beneficial.*

Don't dismiss the idea of trying a work diary because you think you have to create finely-crafted entries for posterity. We've found that if you avoid making a big commitment to it, you'll be more successful. Don't worry about how to express yourself. Simply describe one event or insight from the day. In our study, the average length of the entries was a mere 54 words.

To get started:

- **Pick a time.** Consider when you're most likely to have ten minutes to yourself. Ideally, this will be the same time each day, because it's much easier to get into the habit that way. For some of us, that will be the very end of the day, just before bed. For others, it's at the end of the workday, or on the train ride home.

- **Create a memory trigger.** Choose something you'll see or hear at the designated writing time. For example, if you want to do the diary before you leave the office at 5:00, set a repeating alarm in your calendar for 4:50. If you choose bedtime, put your diary notebook and a pen on your bedside table.

- **Select a medium.** Find something you enjoy using. People have very different preferences for diarykeeping. Some love a leather-bound, monogrammed, silk-bookmarked, five-year diary, with just a few pre-ruled lines for each day. Others like online journaling programs (like iDoneThis). Whether it's a Word doc, a note app, a spiral-bound notebook to an Excel spreadsheet, use whatever works for you.

- **Reflect on your day.** Some people discover what they think as they write, but most of us need a bit of time to collect our thoughts. Use the first three minutes to let your mind go to any one of these types of events from the day:

  - Progress . . . and what led to it. (Congratulate yourself!)

  - Setbacks . . . and what might have caused them. (Learn from them!)

  - Something good. (Feel grateful!)

  - Something difficult. (Get it off your chest!)

  - One thing you can do tomorrow to make your work go better. (Then plan how to do it!)

  - Anything else that dominates your reflection time.

- **Write.** Use the remaining seven minutes to jot down your thoughts. Don't give a thought to grammar, proper sentence construction, style, etc. Focus on the event.

- **Review.** Once in a while, take a few minutes to sit down with your journal and a favorite beverage in a comfy chair. Much of the value in a diary comes from periodically reviewing the past few days (or more).

Keep a diary for just one project, for just a few weeks, and you might find it's a productivity tool you don't want to give up.

Teresa Amabile is the Edsel Bryant Ford Professor of Business Administration at Harvard Business School. She researches what makes people creative, productive, happy, and motivated at work. **Steven Kramer** is a psychologist and independent researcher. They are coauthors of *The Progress Principle* (Harvard Business Review Press, 2011).

Section 6
Renew Your Energy

Chapter 21
How to Accomplish More by Doing Less

by Tony Schwartz

We know that it's not just the number of hours we sit at our desks that determines the value we generate. It's the energy and focus we bring to those hours. Human beings are designed to pulse rhythmically between spending and renewing energy. That's how we operate at our best. Maintaining a steady reservoir of energy—physically, mentally, emotionally, and even spiritually—requires refueling intermittently.

Take for example, two people of equal skill—Bill and Nick—who work in the same office. Each day they arrive at work at 9:00 AM and leave at 7:00 PM.

Adapted from content posted on hbr.org on December 13, 2011.

Bill works for 10 hours—essentially without stop-ping—juggling tasks at his desk and running between meetings all day long. He even eats lunch at his desk. By 1:00 PM, Bill's feeling tired and beginning to lose focus. Between 4:00 and 7:00 PM, he's really dragging and eas-ily distracted.

It's the **law of diminishing returns.** Because he doesn't take breaks to renew his energy, Bill effectively delivers about 6 hours of productive work over his 10-hour day—about 60% of his capacity.

Now contrast that with Nick. He puts in the same 10 hours as Bill. But rather than working essentially with-out stopping, Nick paces himself: he works intensely for approximately 90 minutes at a stretch, and then takes a 15-minute break before resuming work. At 12:15, he goes out for lunch for 45 minutes or works out in a nearby gym. At 3:00 PM, he goes out to his car and takes a brief rest. Sometimes it turns into a 15- or 20-minute nap. Fi-nally, between 4:30 and 5:00, he takes a 15-minute walk outside.

Nick takes off a total of two hours during his 10 at work, so he "only" puts in 8 hours. But because he's build-ing in periods of renewal with scheduled breaks, he's able to work at 80% percent of his full capacity over the course of the whole day—**20% more than Bill.**

Cycling through periods of work and rest allows Nick to be more focused and alert than Bill, to make fewer mistakes, and to return home at night with more energy left for his family.

Work the way Nick does, and you'll get more done, in less time, at a higher level of quality, more sustainably.

Learn how to **manage your energy, not your time,** in the next article.

———————

Tony Schwartz is the president and CEO of The Energy Project and the author of *Be Excellent at Anything*. Become a fan of The Energy Project on Facebook and connect with Tony on Twitter at @tonyschwartz and @energy_project.

Chapter 22
Manage Your Energy, Not Your Time

A summary of the full-length HBR article by **Tony Schwartz** *and* **Catherine McCarthy,** *highlighting key ideas.*

THE IDEA IN BRIEF

Is your job demanding more from you than ever before? Do you feel as if you're working additional hours but rarely getting ahead? Is your mobile device leashing you to your job 24/7? Do you feel exhausted, disengaged, sick?

Spending longer days at the office and putting in extra hours at home doesn't work because your time is a limited resource. But your personal energy is renewable. By fostering deceptively simple **rituals** that will help you regularly replenish your energy, you can strengthen your physical, emotional, mental, and spiritual resilience. These rituals include taking brief breaks at specific intervals, expressing appreciation to others, reducing interruptions, and spending more time on the activities you do best and enjoy most.

THE IDEA IN PRACTICE

Try these practices to renew the four dimensions of your personal energy:

Physical Energy

- Enhance your sleep by setting an earlier bedtime and reducing alcohol use.

- Reduce stress by engaging in cardiovascular activity at least three times a week and strength training at least once a week.

- Eat small meals and light snacks every three hours.

- Learn to notice signs of imminent flagging energy, including restlessness, yawning, hunger, and difficulty concentrating.

- Take brief but regular breaks away from your desk at 90- to 120-minute intervals throughout the day.

Emotional Energy

- Defuse negative emotions—irritability, impatience, anxiety, insecurity—through deep abdominal breathing.

- Fuel positive emotions in yourself and others by regularly expressing appreciation to people in detailed, specific terms through notes, e-mails, calls, or conversations.

- Look at upsetting situations through new lenses. Adopt a **reverse lens** to ask, "What would the other person in this conflict say, and how might he be right?" Use a **long lens** to ask, "How will I likely view this situation in six months?" Employ a **wide lens** to ask, "How can I grow and learn from this situation?"

Mental Energy

- Reduce interruptions by performing high-concentration tasks away from phones and e-mail.

- Respond to voice mails and e-mails at designated times during the day.

- Select the most important challenge for the next day the night before. Then make that challenge your first priority when you arrive at work in the morning.

Spiritual Energy

- Identify your "sweet spot" activities—those that give you feelings of effectiveness, effortless absorption, and fulfillment. Find ways to do more of these. One executive who hated doing sales reports delegated them to someone who loved that activity.

- Allocate time and energy to what you consider most important. For example, spend the last 20 minutes of your evening commute relaxing, so you can connect with your family once you're home.

- Live your core values. For instance, if being considerate is important to you but you're perpetually late for meetings, practice intentionally showing up five minutes early for meetings.

Are You Headed for an Energy Crisis?

Take the following quiz to identify which areas of your life could benefit from energy-renewing rituals.

Please check the statements below that are true for you:

Body

☐ I don't regularly get at least seven to eight hours of sleep, and I often wake up feeling tired.

☐ I frequently skip breakfast, or I settle for something that isn't nutritious.

☐ I don't work out enough (meaning cardiovascular training at least three times a week and strength training at least once a week).

☐ I don't take regular breaks during the day to renew and recharge, or I often eat lunch at my desk, if I eat it at all.

Emotions

- ☐ I frequently find myself feeling irritable, impatient, or anxious at work, especially when work is demanding.

- ☐ I don't have enough time with my family and loved ones, and when I'm with them, I'm not always *really* with them.

- ☐ I have too little time for the activities that I most deeply enjoy.

- ☐ I don't stop frequently enough to express my appreciation to others or to savor my accomplishments and blessings.

Mind

- ☐ I have difficulty focusing on one thing at a time, and I am easily distracted during the day, especially by e-mail.

- ☐ I spend much of my day reacting to immediate crises and demands rather than focusing on activities with longer-term value and high leverage.

- ☐ I don't take enough time for reflection, strategizing, and creative thinking.

- ☐ I often work in the evenings or on weekends, and I almost never take an e-mail–free vacation.

Spirit

- ☐ I don't spend enough time at work doing what I do best and enjoy most.

☐ There are significant gaps between what I say is most important to me and how I actually allocate my time and energy.

☐ My decisions at work are more often influenced by external demands than by a strong, clear sense of my own purpose.

☐ I don't invest enough time and energy in making a positive difference to others or to the world.

How Is Your Overall Energy?

Total number of statements checked: _____

Guide to energy scores

0–3: Excellent energy management skills

4–6: Reasonable energy management skills

7–10: Significant energy management deficits

11–16: A full-fledged energy management crisis

What Do You Need to Work On?

Number of checks in each category:

Body _____

Mind _____

Emotions _____

Spirit _____

Guide to category scores

0: Excellent energy management skills

1: Strong energy management skills

2: Significant deficits

3: Poor energy management skills

4: A full-fledged energy crisis

———————

Tony Schwartz (tony@theenergyproject.com) is the president and CEO of The Energy Project in New York City, and a coauthor of *The Power of Full Engagement: Managing Energy, Not Time, Is the Key to High Performance and Personal Renewal* (Free Press, 2003).

Catherine McCarthy (catherine@theenergyproject.com) is a senior vice president at The Energy Project.

Chapter 23
Why Great Performers Sleep More

by Tony Schwartz

Why is sleep one of the first things we're willing to sacrifice as the demands in our lives keep rising? We continue to live by a remarkably durable myth: Sleeping one hour less will give us one more hour of productivity. In reality, even small amounts of sleep deprivation take a significant toll on our health, mood, cognitive capacity, and productivity.

How Much Sleep Do You Need?

When researchers put test subjects into environments without clocks or windows and ask them to sleep any

---

Adapted from content posted on hbr.org on March 3, 2011.

time they feel tired, 95% sleep between seven and eight hours out of every 24. Another 2.5% sleep more than eight hours. That means just 2.5% of us require fewer than seven hours of sleep a night to feel fully rested. That's one out of every 40 people.

In my talks, when I ask who has had fewer than seven hours of sleep several nights during the past week, the majority raise their hands. That's true whether it's an audience of corporate executives, teachers, cops, or government workers.

Great performers are an exception. Typically, they sleep significantly *more* than the rest of us. In Anders Ericsson's famous study of violinists, the top performers slept an average of eight and a half hours out of every 24, including a 20- to 30-minute midafternoon nap—some two hours a day more than the average American.

The top violinists also reported that except for practice itself, sleep was the most important factor in improving their skills.

As I gathered research about sleep, I felt increasingly compelled to give it higher priority in my own life. Today, I go to great lengths to ensure that I get at least eight hours every night, and ideally between eight and a half and nine hours, even when I'm traveling.

I still take the overnight redeye from California to New York, but I'm asleep by takeoff—even if I have to take a sleeping aid. When I get home at 6:00 or 7:00 AM, I go right to bed until I've had my eight hours. What I've learned about those days is that I'd rather work at 100% for five or six hours than at 60% for eight or nine hours.

With sufficient sleep, I feel better, I work with more focus, and I manage my emotions better, which is good for

WHAT PEOPLE ARE SAYING ON HBR.ORG

Try the coffee nap—Lifehacker had a great article about [naps]. I'm a paramedic and I've used this trick for ages. Fix a cup of coffee so you can drink it quickly. Set up the spot where you'll nap and then drink the coffee. Set a timer for 20 minutes and make sure you get up when it goes off. Any longer and you'll feel worn out. I know this has saved my life on many late-night, long-distance transports. —Posted by John

everyone around me. I dislike enduring even a single day when I haven't had enough sleep because the impact is immediate and unavoidable. On the rare days that I don't get enough, I try hard to get at least a 20- to 30-minute nap in the afternoon. That's a big help.

How to Get More Sleep

Here are three other tips to improve the quantity and quality of your sleep:

- **Write down what's on your mind before you get into bed.** If you leave items such as unfinished to-do's and unresolved issues in your working memory, they'll make it harder to fall asleep, and you'll end up ruminating about them if you wake up during the night.

- **Go to bed earlier—and at a set time.** Sounds obvious, right? The problem is there's no alternative. You're already waking up at the latest possible time you can. If you don't ritualize a specific bedtime, you'll find ways to stay up later, just the way you do now.

- **Start winding down at least 45 minutes before you turn out the light.** You won't fall asleep if you're all wound up from answering e-mail or doing other work. Create a ritual around drinking a cup of herbal tea, listening to music that helps you relax, or reading a dull book.

————————

Tony Schwartz is the president and CEO of The Energy Project and the author of *Be Excellent at Anything.* Become a fan of The Energy Project on Facebook and connect with Tony on Twitter at @tonyschwartz and @energy_project.

Section 7:
Take Control of Your E-mail

Chapter 24
Simplify Your E-mail

by Gina Trapani

If you spend more time dealing with e-mail than getting the right work done, it's time for an e-mail makeover.

Clear Out Your In-Box

Computer scientists developed e-mail based on the paradigm of postal mail, so think of your in-box like your physical mailbox. You wouldn't keep bills you have to pay and the invitation to that birthday party in there forever, right? Sort by sender, date, or subject line to clear out your messages as efficiently as possible. Then delete the junk; unsubscribe from newsletters you never read or websites you no longer visit. If you have thousands of messages in your main folder, business writer Amy Gallo

---

Adapted from content posted on hbr.org on June 9, 2009.

suggests creating a new subfolder in your Archive folder called "Old In-box" and putting all of your messages in there. You'll still have access to them if you need them, but you'll be able to jump-start your new e-mail process without the drudgery of actually reviewing every old message.

Set Up Just Three Folders

Sometimes it's not just the sheer volume of messages that makes e-mail management a time-sink, it's the complicated folder system we've concocted. Streamline your in-box by creating these three folders:

Follow-up: For messages you have to respond to or act on that will take longer than a couple of minutes. (Put a corresponding item on your to-do list for each of these messages.)

Hold: For messages where you're waiting for something to happen, like a package shipment or event invitation. (Put a corresponding item on your calendar for each of these messages.)

Archive: For messages you're done with but want to keep for reference.

Maintain Your New System

Once you've cleaned out your in-box, you'll want to keep it organized and manageable, so you can focus your attention on your most important work.

Here are some techniques to keep your e-mail under control:

- **Process your e-mail in batches.** Most of us are on
  e-mail all day, scanning for anything urgent and ignoring everything else, which is how backlog accu-
  mulates in your in-box. Instead of checking every
  time you hear the incoming message "ding," process your e-mail in batches. Completely shut down
  your e-mail or set it and your handheld to check
  for messages only every few hours. Then, when you
  have time or are in between tasks, fully commit
  yourself to processing new messages. Alexandra
  Samuel, cofounder of Social Signal, recommends
  selecting specific times when you'll process e-mail
  (for example, 8:00 to 10:00 AM and 4:00 to
  6:00 PM). Notify correspondents and colleagues
  of your schedule through your e-mail signature or
  a note on your blog (and clear this approach with
  your supervisor, if applicable). Assume that if it's
  an emergency, people will call you—but refrain
  from actually suggesting that, since you don't want
  to encourage a constantly ringing phone.

- **Use the "two-minute" rule.** As you process your
  e-mail in batches, reply to any messages that will
  take fewer than two minutes on the spot. Don't de-
  lay and leave them in your in-box marked as read,
  thinking you'll get back to them; don't even file
  them away in "Follow-up." Just take care of them
  immediately. To help keep you within the two-
  minute mark, try answering all e-mails in three
  sentences or fewer (visit **Three.Sentenc.es**), says
  Dave Kerpen, CEO of Likeable Media. Anything

that takes more text probably requires a quick call instead. Have your team or department try this as a group experiment, and watch your collective e-mail–processing time shrink.

- **End "Reply all."** Kerpen also recommends using internal social networking tools instead of e-mail to chat with your coworkers, facilitate collaboration and passive listening, and eliminate the dreaded "Reply all" e-mail chains. Try a private, closed Facebook group. Or explore proprietary tools such as **Jive** and **Yammer**, which allow organizations to set up private social networking platforms. Jive is best for large enterprises, while Yammer is suitable for departments or smaller organizations. Get an on-the-spot answer and get on with your work.

- **Stop spamming people.** Samuel notes that a major contributor to e-mail overload is the widely held expectation that every e-mail must get a reply, even if it's just "OK" or "Thanks." Don't do it.

For more suggestions on keeping your e-mail under control, see the next article, "Eight E-mail Overload Experiments."

———————

Gina Trapani is the founding editor of the personal productivity blog Lifehacker.com.

Chapter 25
Eight E-mail Overload Experiments

by Alexandra Samuel

If you've tried all of the basic ways to structure and manage your e-mail, but are still feeling overwhelmed, here are eight road-tested experiments for battling e-mail overload that range from reasonable to radical. Try each one, or a couple at a time—but push yourself to the very limits of your comfort zone, because the tactics that seem most inconceivable may be just the ones that help you discover a new way to work more effectively with e-mail.

If your company's culture includes expecting instant replies to every message, e-mail your colleagues and regular correspondents to let them know about your experiment. This will help avoid ruffled feathers over some of the more radical suggestions.

1. **Reject the mandatory reply.** Set up an auto-responder that lets all correspondents know that you're only replying to selected e-mail, depending on your availability and priorities—and make it clear you don't expect a reply to every e-mail you send them, either.

   Here's one version:

   SUBJECT: Limited e-mail means I may not reply to the message you sent

   Thank you for getting in touch. I'm experimenting with a new approach to e-mail: I'm sending and replying to a smaller number of messages. I still check e-mail regularly, so if you don't get a reply within 72 hours please assume I have reviewed and filed your message. This approach should help me focus my attention on my current priorities. Thank you for your understanding.

   For a less extreme solution, add a polite line to your standard e-mail signature. Here's mine:

   Alexandra Samuel, PhD
   Director, Social + Interactive Media Centre,
   Emily Carr University
   alex@alexandrasamuel.com |
   Twitter @awsamuel
   Join the fight against e-mail overload:
   - Focus on *your* priorities; I'll understand if you don't reply.
   - Sorry if I don't reply; I'm trying to focus, too.
   - If it's urgent, reach me by Twitter or SMS.

2. **Set message quotas.** For outbound messages, limit the number of e-mail threads you initiate each day. Assume that every e-mail you send will generate 4–10 responses, so you're creating work for yourself with each message. Send fewer, and you'll get fewer. For incoming messages, guesstimate the number and make that your daily quota. Use filters in your e-mail software to sort incoming mail and keep all but the most crucial messages out of your in-box. Auto-file other messages in alternative folders. Keep adding rules until your daily in-box volume falls below the quota you've set.

   For example, I automatically direct e-mails into different folders for internal mail, messages I'm cc'd on, social network notifications, and more. My closest colleagues know that any e-mail marked "URGENT" still comes directly to my in-box; you might set your rules to ensure that all messages from your boss come through marked as high priority or color coded in a way that makes them stand out. The filters thin the incoming messages to a manageable level and ensure that e-mails from current or prospective clients don't get lost in a sea of spam.

3. **Reply by phone.** You can eliminate dozens of e-mails a day with quick calls. A five-minute chat about a landmine your project just stumbled on may be more efficient than crafting an

e-mail that adequately explains the situation. Also, thank people in person or by phone, even if that means leaving a voice mail (detailed thanks for project work, however, should always go by e-mail, so the recipient can file it for performance reviews). Most crucially, switch to phone or in-person communication whenever you get a message that angers or hurts you, because e-mail exchanges tend to escalate and solidify grievances.

4. **Do not copy.** Refuse to send, read, or reply to cc'ed messages. As blogging entrepreneur Anil Dash puts it, including someone as a cc on an e-mail is like saying "This is important enough for me to interrupt you [with] but not to write to you [about directly]." If a message you're sending requires a recipient's attention, include that person in the "to" field; if not, leave them off entirely. Tell colleagues they should address messages to you directly if they need you to reply.

5. **Don't touch that phone!** When you have a few minutes between meetings or while waiting for a plane, don't use that time to respond to e-mail on your mobile's tiny keyboard. Rather than send a rash or typo-ridden reply, wait until you're back at your desk or with your laptop or tablet, when you can craft a better response in less time.

6. **Take an e-mail vacation:** Try a two-week vacation, a six-month sabbatical, or something in between. But it's not much of a break if you come back to an overflowing in-box, so before you tune out, turn on the vacation auto-responder with a message like this:

Thanks for your message. I'm taking an e-mail vacation until the new year. The message you've just sent me has been filed, so it's not lost forever, but if you need a reply it would be great if you could e-mail me sometime on or after January 4. If you need to reach me urgently, I'll be available by Twitter or mobile phone.

Set your e-mail program to file everything in a folder labeled "Vacation," and when you return, take a quick look for any truly life-changing messages you may have missed and actively ignore the rest. If someone really wants to reach you, they'll e-mail again.

7. **Reply to *every* e-mail:** If ignoring e-mail makes your palms sweat, maybe it's time to give into its primacy. For two weeks, make your *entire morning* an e-mail processing zone. (If three hours isn't enough, block as big a chunk of time as you think you'll need.) See whether your commitment to a 100% response rate makes you more effective. This will help you make some conscious decisions about how

to better allocate your time and triage your in-box.

8. **Give up e-mail altogether:** For the ultimate in in-box liberation, give it up. Yes, you really can—especially if you're comfortable with social media tools. Use your blog to post updates on your work instead of sending an e-mail to a big distribution list; Basecamp or another project management tool to communicate with project teams; Google Docs to circulate drafts; Skype for a quick conversation instead of a 14-message exchange; and Twitter DMs, chat, and SMS for tight, efficient, and confidential messaging. Take your e-mail address off your business card and Web page, and encourage anyone who needs to reach you to pick up the phone.

Alexandra Samuel is the Director of the Social + Interactive Media Centre at Emily Carr University, and the cofounder of Social Signal, a Vancouver-based social media agency. You can follow Alex on Twitter at @awsamuel or her blog at alexandrasamuel.com.

Section 8
Maintain Your New Approach

Chapter 26
Sustaining Your Productivity System

by Alexandra Samuel

A productivity system is like any other faith: It works for as long as you continue to believe in it. Let a hint of skepticism creep in—about the discipline required, the rewards promised, or the potential superiority of other ideologies—and the threat of disorder quickly returns.

If you can accept that your system is a work in progress, it's a lot easier to keep that threat at bay. Here are some tips for sustaining your productivity system:

1. **Focus on outcomes.** Many productivity methodologies are so specific about their recommended processes that your zeal for maintaining your folders, sorting your communications,

or acquiring snazzy storage bins can easily eclipse the problems or benefits that motivated you in the first place. Remember that adherence to a system is a false god: Don't stick to it just because you bought the book or the software. If you're working effectively and meeting your deadlines, it doesn't matter if you no longer geocode your task list.

2. **Make micro commitments.** When you embrace a new productivity religion, adopt its minor practices as well as its major ones. Sometimes the smaller commitments are the most sustainable. For example, two years after I got serious about In-box Zero, I no longer process my in-box to empty *every day*. But my e-mail is still dramatically easier to manage, thanks to the various filters I initially set up as part of my in-box zero approach.

3. **Find fellow adherents.** One of my big stumbling blocks with David Allen's book *Getting Things Done* was Allen's denunciation of hanging folders; my file cabinet *only* worked with hanging files. Happily, I thought to Google "GTD hanging files," and discovered a community of enthusiasts discussing the merits of various folder styles—and even brands—with the seriousness of Talmudic scholars. Reading about how other people implemented and adjusted the system liberated me from my slavish

adherence to every detail. You can also *make*
your own adherents: Marnie Webb, the CEO of
nonprofit tech resource CompuMentor/
TechSoup, keeps a shelf full of copies of *Getting
Things Done*. "When one of my team members
complains about not being able to manage
their lists or having too much to do, I pull a
book off my shelf," Webb says. "I tell them to
complain again after they've implemented
[GTD] for three months."

4. **Schedule routine maintenance.** A few years ago
   I sorted all the junk in our home office into
   beautifully labeled boxes. Six months later, a
   friend observed that whether you opened a
   box labeled "Bills to Pay" or "Pens and High-
   lighters," you were guaranteed to find a pad of
   Post-its, an iPod adapter, a handful of bat-
   teries, and 37 cents in change. Now I know
   that *getting* organized isn't enough—to *stay*
   organized, I have to set aside a couple of days
   every 4–6 months so that I can reestablish
   order and update my systems. (This is one of
   my favorite ways to make productive use of the
   few days after a major trip or project wrap-up,
   when I'm too brain-dead to do anything more
   demanding.)

5. **Anticipate obsolescence.** Even the best productivity systems and tips may not survive
   the passage of time and the advent of new

technologies. So stick with software tools that provide options for exporting your data to .csv, iCal, or other standard formats, so you don't get trapped by any one platform.

6. **Embrace eclecticism.** Troy Angrignon, vice president of sales and marketing at Cloudscaling, is religious about tracking his tasks and goals using a single, two-column document whose structure borrows from just about every productivity guru out there—Brian Tracy, David Allen, Robert Fritz. While combining approaches might amount to apostasy in the eyes of any one system's adherents, it's allowed Angrignon to develop a customized method that's served him well for 15 years, even as he continues to make adjustments and sample new tools. You may also find that tweaking your productivity system, whether it's trying out a new calendaring approach or sorting your paper files, is part of your creative process—a way of preparing yourself for a new year or project.

Alexandra Samuel is the Director of the Social + Interactive Media Centre at Emily Carr University, and the co-founder of Social Signal, a Vancouver-based social media agency. You can follow Alex on Twitter at @awsamuel or her blog at alexandrasamuel.com.

Section 9
Explore Further

Chapter 27
More Productivity Books to Explore

by Ilan Mochari

This guide provides a wide range of tactics and tips for improving your productivity. If you wish to explore further, we've summarized the approaches of three other experts: Stephen Covey, Julie Morgenstern, and David Allen.

The Seven Habits of Highly Effective People, by Stephen R. Covey

The Basic Idea: This is a guide to changing your life, not just the way you manage your day. To zero in on the best ways to spend your time and energy, focus on things you can control, keep your desired outcomes (for both individual projects and your life overall) in mind, improve your personal and professional relationships, nurture yourself, and classify your tasks as urgent or important.

Ideal if you:	Not ideal if you:
• Want to transform how you live. For example, you *can* break old habits like procrastination, but it will require work on your character, not just your productivity practices. • Have spiritual leanings and want to develop mission statements for different areas of your life ("I want to raise two self-confident children" or "I'm here to deliver smart and media-savvy public relations services to my customers. I will draw on my industry knowledge, my understanding of my clients and their challenges, and a genuine passion for what I do."). • Enjoy a longer read, rich with personal anecdotes and scholarly references.	• Are happy with your life outside work and simply want a nuts-and-bolts system for managing workflow. • Will roll your eyes at phrases like "opening the gate of change," "emotional bank account," and "abundance mentality." • Are looking for advice that addresses modern worklife and gadgets. Covey's advice transcends trends, but his book predates smartphones and social networking. • Are looking for advice on organizing your physical workspace.

Additional resources: franklincovey.com, stephencovey.com, the3rdalternative.com.

Organizing from the Inside Out,
by Julie Morgenstern

The Basic Idea: This book will help you organize your physical spaces depending on your personality, needs, and goals. Identify the root cause of your clutter (Is your current system too complex? Are you by nature a packrat?). Find homes for your most important things by using the Kindergarten approach: Divide your space into specific activity zones that have everything necessary to do whatever type of work you've assigned to that area, with appropriate supplies and storage units to keep them contained. For example, set up a bill-paying area with everything you need—even if it means duplicates (like postage stamps) in multiple zones.

Ideal if you:	Not ideal if you:
• Literally have trouble finding things. • Want advice about organizing physical spaces (desks, offices, filing systems). • Prefer lists and tips in clearly signposted sections.	• Aren't a fan of self-reflection. • Are looking for more advice about productivity or time management. • Are looking for a quick fix or an excuse to purge everything. Morgenstern recommends a three-step approach (analyzye, strategize, attack), with a five-step process for the attack phase.

Additional resources: juliemorgenstern.com, oprah.com/home/More-with-Organizing-Expert-Julie-Morgenstern, amazon.com/Julie-Morgenstern/e/B001IGQY78

Getting Things Done, by David Allen

The Basic Idea: This book will help you gather, evaluate, and make progress on all of your tasks. Don't rely on your brain to remember everything you have to do. Instead, write it all down in a calendar and series of lists (projects, next actions, waiting for, maybe/someday). Review each task and determine if you should: do it, delegate it, or defer it. When you're ready to start a new task, use four criteria to decide what to do: context, time available, energy available, priority. Once a week, gather your lists and calendar to review your system, update your lists, and check in with yourself about where you are relative to your workload and schedule.

Ideal if you:	Not ideal if you:
• Want a nuts-and-bolts guide to determining priorities and mastering workflow. • Prefer bulleted lists, diagrams, scattered inspirational quotes, and flowcharts. • Have the authority or resources to delegate. • Are looking for advice on setting up physical work spaces, as well as productivity in general.	• Seek spiritual guidance, too. • Enjoy storytelling or personal anecdotes in your business reading. • Are overwhelmed by setting up elaborate physical file-folder systems. • Aren't comfortable delegating.

Additional resources: davidco.com, gtdtimes.com, youtube.com/watch?v=Qo7vUdKTlhk

---

Ilan Mochari is chief writer for *The Build Network* and a contributor to the *MIT Sloan Management Review*.

Chapter 28
Productivity Apps and Tools

Here are some apps and websites to further fuel your interest in making the most of your time and energy. This is by no means an exhaustive list—we've compiled favorites from some of the most productive members of our hbr.org community: Joshua Gans, Skoll Chair in Innovation and Entrepreneurship, Rotman School of Management, University of Toronto; Heidi Grant Halvorson, PhD, author of *Nine Things Successful People Do Differently*; Whitney Johnson, author of *Dare Dream Do*; Dave Kerpen, author of *Likeable Social Media*; and Andrew McAfee, author of *Enterprise 2.0*. Since technology is ever-evolving, consider this an inspiration list. For example, if Longer Days is no longer available when you look for it, try a search for virtual assistant to see what new offerings exist.

Manage Your Schedule

- **Longer Days, Brickwork,** and **Uassist.ME** are just three of dozens of virtual assistant companies that provide online access to people to help with administrative tasks, such as scheduling meetings and calls, researching individuals' backgrounds for networking opportunities, marketing research (such as company information or revenue data); other professional functions, such as copywriting and managing event RSVPs; and even personal tasks like scheduling doctor's appointments. Virtual assistants add extra hands without adding extra headcount. The programs are relatively inexpensive: Longerdays.com offers 20 hours for $350 and Uassist.ME charges $650 per month for about 40 hours/month's worth of work. —*Dave Kerpen*

- **Tungle.Me** and **Doodle** will end those long, painful e-mail chains that often result when you're trying to set up a meeting with multiple people inside and outside of your organization. **Tungle .Me** allows people to see your calendar availability and easily schedule meetings and phone calls, and it syncs with most Web and mobile calendar applications. **Doodle** allows multiple parties to share their availability via poll and quickly find a mutually convenient date and time for an event. —*Dave Kerpen*

Make Your Lists

- **Workflowy** is an online tool and app that allows you to better organize yourself by mimicking the way you naturally think. It helps you make a list of

high-level ideas and tasks and then breaks them into smaller pieces. For example, I've started with Personal and Work as my two broad categories. Under "Work," I've created sublists such as Rose Park Advisors, Book launch, and HBR blog. You can subdivide lists like this almost infinitely.
—*Whitney Johnson*

- **Remember The Milk** is an online task manager that allows you to easily track your to-do list from your smartphone. You can add items to your to-do list, set location tags to help you remember to take care of things when you're out and about, organize tasks by priority, schedule tasks by integrating with popular calendar tools (including Outlook and Google Calendar), and sync everything so that you can see your updated, prioritized list whether you're at your desk or on the go. —*Dave Kerpen*

- **Evernote** allows you to capture notes, files, and images and later access them from your tablet, mobile, or computer through a robust search feature. Save favorite Web pages with notes about them, take a picture of a potential location for a future launch party, record your thoughts on your next product idea and add to it whenever and wherever inspiration strikes, or keep your scanned itineraries and travel docs all in one place. Evernote also makes it easy to share notes and documents with friends, classmates, and colleagues.
—*Dave Kerpen*

Manage Your Reminders

- **Due** is an iPhone app that repeatedly reminds you to do something at a certain time—until you do it. Here's how it works: You need to remember to write an e-mail to someone but can't do it right now. With Due, you set your phone to alert you to write the e-mail at a certain time (30 minutes from now, 4 PM). I used to leave myself notes or write on my hand. With Due, I can do the same thing but with more precision. It will continue to beep until I accept the reminder or change the time I want to be reminded. —*Joshua Gans*

- **Nudge-mail** helps you remember what you need to do when you need to do it. Whether your spouse asks you to pick up milk on your way home or a client requests a draft proposal, Nudge-mail reminds you of the task at the right time. Just forward an e-mail to addresses like "tomorrow@nudge-mail.com" or "2hours@nudge-mail.com" and free your mind to focus on your next important task.
  —*Dave Kerpe*n

Manage Your Files

- If you use multiple computers, work on several projects, and/or have multiple colleagues, try **Dropbox.** It's a cloud-based storage utility that eliminates file-related hassles. It puts your files in one folder that all of your devices can access, and synchronizes them in the background without your having to lift a finger. It also allows you to share different folders with collaborators. How many times have you tried to send a file via e-mail, only to have a server reject it because it was too big? Just create a Dropbox folder, invite the recipient(s) to share it, and your problems are past tense. —*Andrew McAfee*

- **JotNot** is an iPhone app that allows you to take a photo of any image or document and instantly turn it into a .pdf—for example, you can sign and fax back a contract in seconds, on the go. —*Dave Kerpen*

Manage Your Social Media

- I don't know what I would do without **HootSuite.** It's a social media dashboard that allows you to monitor and post to all your networks simulta-neously. If you blog or use social media for your work, this is a *huge* timesaver. When I've written something new or read something I want to share on my networks, I can let everyone know with a single entry, rather than having to log on to each network separately. I use it to manage my Face-book, Twitter, LinkedIn, and Google+ accounts, and you can also use it with Tumblr, WordPress, and Foursquare. —*Heidi Grant Halvorson, PhD*

- **Buffer** allows you to schedule Tweets and Face-book messages (and soon, LinkedIn posts) ahead of time, and automatically spaces them out. In five minutes, you can find interesting articles worth sharing with colleagues and prospective clients, and be tweeting all day, without actually going to Twitter again. —*Dave Kerpen*

- **Rapportive** is a browser add-on for Gmail that transforms Gmail's bland sidebar into a time-saver. Instead of ads, you'll see social media information about the sender of the e-mail: his picture, links to his profile, recent Tweets, etc. The add-on is available for Firefox, Chrome, and Safari, is free to use, and integrates smoothly with Gmail. This tool obviates the need for a separate search to find out more about new contacts or clients.
  —*Dave Kerpen*

- **Dragon Dictation** is a voice-recognition application that allows you to easily dictate text or e-mail messages. Speak into the program and instantly see the transcription. Faster and safer than typing while on the go, you can dictate everything from Tweets to longer e-mail messages. —*Dave Kerpen*

- **NutshellMail** eliminates the need for multiple visits to your social network accounts. It sends you a daily summary and includes only important information such as Facebook likes, posts, and comments; and Twitter mentions, new followers, and Tweets. —*Dave Kerpen*

Index

Index

Index

Notes

Notes

Notes

Notes

Notes

Notes

Notes

Notes

Notes

Notes